To:

....

From:

....

Date:

....

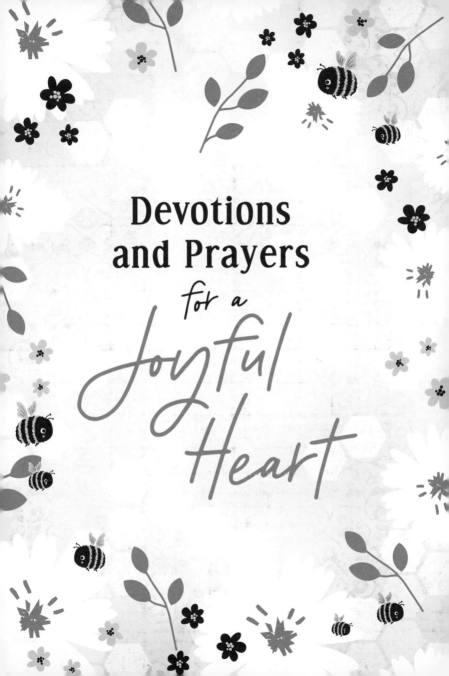

Devotions
and Prayers
for a
Joyful
Heart

Lindsey Miller

Devotions and Prayers

for a

Joyful Heart

Meditations for Women

BARBOUR

PUBLISHING

Published by Barbour Publishing, Inc., 1810 Barbour Drive, Uhrichsville, Ohio 44683, www.barbourbooks.com

Our mission is to inspire the world with the life-changing message of the Bible.

ecpa Member of the Evangelical Christian Publishers Association

Printed in China.

Introduction

When was the last time you woke up happy, not dreading the uncertain day ahead but filled with joy and hope for what God has in store for you? Considering the numerous hardships in today's world, it's probably been awhile. It's impossible to turn on the television and not stumble across bad news. Between that and your daily life struggles, it's no wonder you wake up with anxiety.

It's easy to get so distracted by our very existence that we forget God is in control. The Creator has great plans for you—and His plans don't include living day to day without hope for your future. Our days might be uncertain, but God abides. He sits on the throne. He cares for His children. His plans for you are good!

This devotional is meant to awaken that sleeping part of you that may have forgotten who you are—a child of God! You are here because of His love. He created you. He knows you inside and out. He loves you unconditionally. So regardless of where you find yourself, whatever your circumstance might be, remember that you always have a reason to shout for joy!

The Perfect Storm

For God is not a God of confusion but of peace.
1 CORINTHIANS 14:33 ESV

. . . .

Imagine yourself on a boat. The rain starts and doesn't stop. The thunder grows louder. The wind fiercer. The waves bigger. You find yourself holding on to anything that won't be washed away by the next wave. Then you hear a voice say, "Quiet, be still." Almost immediately, the thunder quiets. The rain stops. The wind ceases. Jesus had spoken to the storm, and it obeyed. The disciples were in awe.

Many times, the feelings you harbor are far more devastating than a storm. When a tempest is raging inside you, it can be hard to know what to cling to. Waves of hopelessness and despair threaten to drown you. A fog clouds your mind, and you lose sight of where to go.

In your despair, reach for the one who doesn't know confusion. Begin with the one who has the authority to calm the disturbance inside you. Dive deeper into the presence of the Lord, and your confusion will pass. Even when you're bewildered by the chaos, you can have joy because God is working His peace. When He speaks, listen.

. . . .

*Lord, I can't deal with the barrage of emotions
I feel right now. You have the authority to calm me,
to bring me peace. I will delight and rest in You.*

No Dotted Line

*He has saved us and called us to a holy life—
not because of anything we have done but because
of his own purpose and grace. This grace was given
us in Christ Jesus before the beginning of time.*

2 TIMOTHY 1:9 NIV

If someone told you that right now, you could obtain that *one thing* you've always wanted, how would you respond? Besides being completely elated, you'd probably wonder if there was a catch. *What do I have to do in return? What will this really cost me?*

From a young age, you were taught to not only say thank you but to always return a kindness or favor. A proper exchange must take place. When you were young, you had to do your chores before you played. As you became an adult, you completed your work before getting a paycheck. So when it comes to receiving gifts, you probably have a natural desire to repay the gift giver in some way—and that's just with gifts that you can see and touch.

There are some gifts that you can't see or touch—like grace. Because of Jesus, God's grace becomes available when you believe in Him. It's there, ready for the taking. The only difficulty comes if you think you somehow need to earn it. With grace, there are no stipulations, conditions, contracts, limitations, or dotted lines awaiting your signature.

You can take joy in accepting God's gift—no catch!

*Lord, I sometimes pay too much attention to what I
"feel" I must do. Thank You for Your grace that shines
on me regardless. I will rejoice in Your love.*

Now You See It

You will show me the way of life. Being with You is to be
full of joy. In Your right hand there is happiness forever.

. . . .

Good magicians never reveal their secrets. They spend years—decades, even—perfecting their craft. It takes great skill to master their sleights of hand. With their magic wands, they can make objects appear, disappear, and even levitate.

No matter how hard you try, though, there's no amount of expertise that can magically erase reality. Sure, you sometimes wish you could say "Abracadabra!" and watch as a mysterious force swoops in and dissipates your worries and stress. But if that were true, you would miss out on so much.

God has made a way for you to have the fullness of joy, even when life gets messy. He has no tricks. No hidden agendas. God has you in His hands, and He doesn't have anything up His sleeve. He just wants your company: only then can He impart immense joy to you right where you are. Not later, not tomorrow—right now!

. . . .

Father God, I'm so grateful that You don't keep secrets
from me. I've been searching for answers—when I really
need to entrust the outcome to You. Thank You for the joy
that comes from knowing my future is in Your hands.

Fan the Flames

*Finally, brothers and sisters, whatever is true, whatever
is noble, whatever is right, whatever is pure, whatever
is lovely, whatever is admirable—if anything is
excellent or praiseworthy—think about such things.*
PHILIPPIANS 4:8 NIV

Vineyard owners work hard to manage their crops. Fresh grapes on the vine must not get cold. Just one freeze is enough to damage the grape clusters and negatively impact the harvest. This can be a real challenge, especially during an unexpected cold snap.

To help combat this, vineyard owners use large paraffin candles, which they light between each row of grapes. Sometimes, if the temperature falls too low, they run fans as well. These fans help circulate the heat, preventing frost from forming around the grape clusters.

Joy works the same way. Radiating pure joy doesn't come naturally for us humans—it takes hard work. You have a choice: to either focus on what's lousy and frustrating or thank God for your blessings. God invites you to fan the warm flames of joy. While it's much easier to dwell on how things could go wrong, the blessings that flow from focusing on the lovely are endless.

*Father God, I'm so sorry for zeroing in on all that is
wrong. You have given me so much to be grateful for.
Thank You for helping me see what is right and good so
that the flames of my joy will burn steady and warm.*

More Than a Feeling

The heart is deceitful above all things, and
desperately sick; who can understand it?
JEREMIAH 17:9 ESV

• •

People react differently when their favorite song comes on the radio. You may get up and dance, use the closest object as a microphone, or—if you're driving—pull over to the side of the road because you can't concentrate on anything else. Hearing your favorite song makes you smile because you know every lyric and note. You sing along, unconcerned about whether you're on key. The right music can get your day off to a great start and even add a noticeable pep to your step.

Unlike the radio, your heart plays songs that are slightly less well known. The rise and fall—joys and sorrows—that your heart can take are sometimes unexpected. The music of your heart can leave you feeling upbeat, devastated, or sad. So it's important that you choose where your attention goes. The focal point of your attention can greatly impact the song of your heart.

Joy must be a focus before it becomes a feeling. Emotions are directly tied to our moods, circumstances, and relationships. All these things can change at a moment's notice. But God *never* changes, and His love for you is more than a feeling.

• •

Lord, I've been listening to the song my heart plays. While
the feelings I have may be confusing, I choose to focus on
who You are and the blessings You've given me.

What Year Is It?

A heart at peace gives life to the body,
but envy rots the bones.
PROVERBS 14:30 NIV

It's the 1950s, and Patricia is heading to a dinner party. The dinner party she threw last week was a huge success, and everyone commented on her lovely roast beef. As she walks in the door, she notices the magnificent spread of food on the table. She spots roast beef—and it looks even more delicious than hers. She is devastated.

It's the 1990s, and Lauren goes outside to ride her bike. She notices her friends are all gathered in Ashley's driveway. As she gets closer, her jaw drops. Ashley has a Gameboy. Lauren's stomach sinks as her envy begins to swell.

It's 2022. Harper opens Facebook and reviews her new friend requests. As she scrolls, she sees something from her friend Chloe. Chloe's employer has sent her to Paris, and she has posted a picture of her looking amazing right next to the Eiffel Tower. Harper feels defeated and starts to tear up.

No matter what year it is, each day brings opportunities to compare yourself to others—especially now, when the intricacies of people's lives rest right at your fingertips. But don't fall into that trap—God's plan for you is far better than anything posted on social media!

Father God, I'm sorry for reducing my joy by comparing
myself to others. I praise You for all You've given me!

Mud Pies

"Fear not, little flock, for it is your Father's good pleasure to give you the kingdom."
LUKE 12:32 ESV

Small children love to play with sticks and mud. In their heads, they are building grand castles, painting masterpieces, and making the most delicious pies. Even though they are completely filthy, they feel accomplished and happy.

You can spend your whole life trying to recapture simple moments like that. You can go to great lengths to create a deep-down feeling of joy. There's nothing wrong with this. But the only foolproof way to create joy in your heart is trusting God and His Word. The Bible promises many rewards, and satisfaction is guaranteed. Any human effort to elicit joy pales in comparison to the Bible's lasting promises and rewards.

It's time to put down your muddy sticks and stop thinking that your creation is the pinnacle of joy. Never settle. There should be no question in your mind that God wants the very best for you. Embrace the lasting happiness and contentment that His grace and truth provide.

Father God, thank You for wanting me to be happy.
Thank You for putting desires in my heart for a reason—
desires that will help grow Your kingdom.

The Bad Guy

*When what is right and fair is done, it is a
joy for those who are right with God.*

PROVERBS 21:15 NLV

. . . .

The popcorn is popping, the soda is fizzing, and the bags of candy are all opened and ready to be enjoyed. You are about to press PLAY and watch one of your favorite movies. It's the one where the hero almost gets overtaken by the bad guy. . .but then conquers him in the end.

It's fun to watch "good versus evil" movies like these. You feel great satisfaction when it ends. Not only did the villain get what he deserved, the hero has served justice and walks away satisfied. All wrongs have been righted. After all the struggle, pain, and loss, peace and happiness prevail.

Unfortunately, reality doesn't usually mimic a movie. It might seem like the bad guys are always winning, and your brain can't compute how evil seems to gain the upper hand. This, however, is not your problem to solve.

The proverbial bad guy will never experience the joy that comes with having integrity. Status or success that's achieved through dishonest means will not last. Continue clinging to God's promises and let Him handle your enemies—both real and perceived. When the credits roll to the story of your life, you too will be satisfied.

. . . .

*Lord Jesus, only You can satisfy my need for justice. I will
remain steadfast in Your presence because You are my joy.*

Gratifying Praise

Praise the LORD! Praise God in his sanctuary;
praise him in his mighty heaven! Praise him for his
mighty works; praise his unequaled greatness!
PSALM 150:1–2 NLT

• •

The Sistine Chapel's ceiling is a magnificent work of art by famous painter Michelangelo. People travel from all over the world to partake in its grandeur. People of all ages and ethnicities can be found inside the chapel, witnessing what many see only in books. Even after five hundred years, the Sistine Chapel continues to awe its patrons.

Do you think that immediately after people witness the beauty of Michelangelo's work, they just continue about their day as usual? Doubtful. It's more likely that they pepper their normal activities—going to the park, meeting a friend for dinner, stopping at the grocery store—with excited proclamations of their experience to anyone who will listen. As they describe how marvelous and beautiful it was, happiness surges within their hearts. In sharing their experience with others, their joy overflows.

Similarly, when the Bible instructs you to praise God, it's not just for Him—it's for you too. When you take a moment to praise Him, it fills you with joy. Whatever your day may hold, a piece of it can be acknowledged and given back to God. Praise may seem like an obligation, but it's intended for your gratification.

Praise Him today!

• •

God, You are so amazing and wonderful. I will praise Your
name daily so that my joy may be complete in You.

17

When the Wind Blows

*As sorrowful, yet always rejoicing; as poor, yet making
many rich; as having nothing, yet possessing everything.*
2 CORINTHIANS 6:10 ESV

. . . .

Technology has made it super easy to prepare yourself for weather of all kinds, but there's nothing wrong with just looking out the window. A simple glance can tell you if it's snowy, rainy, windy, or sunny. From there, you may choose a winter coat, rain jacket, or sundress. While unexpected weather might still happen, you can usually be prepared.

Unfortunately, there is no app or window that shows what the day will hold for you emotionally. When it comes to life, there's no way of knowing when the next storm will hit.

Focusing on joy is like choosing your attire based on the weather. Even if you feel sorrowful or dejected, you can still have joy. Because of God's sufficiency, comfort, and forgiveness, you can be completely joyous in Him—no matter which way the wind blows.

. . . .

*Father God, life has thrown me some unwelcomed stormy
weather. Yet I will praise and bless Your name in the
midst of it because my joy is in You and You alone.*

Raging Joy

*"For my name's sake I defer my anger; for the
sake of my praise I restrain it for you."*
<small>ISAIAH 48:9 ESV</small>

• •

It doesn't matter who or what made you mad—here you are, furious.
You're so angry that if you were a cartoon, flames would be shooting
from your ears. And even though the Bible explains that God will take
care of your enemies, that doesn't satisfy your wish for an immediate
"reckoning." While you may not describe yourself as a creative person,
your fantasies at this moment would suggest otherwise. Countless
scenarios rush through your head—so many conversations where, with
one verbal twist of the knife, you bring your opponents to their knees.
Nothing can squelch your desire for justice.

But as angry as you are, you can be equally as joyful! This is because
you serve a God who will fight your battles better than you ever could.
Oftentimes, you won't get to see your idea of vengeance carried out.
This is for your benefit. Because of human nature, worldly justice will
never be enough. The closure you need can only be found in Jesus. So
if you feel you need to vent your anger, let it be replaced with joy. God
knows. God sees. God cares. And He is far more creative than you.

• •

*Father God, I know You saw what happened and
are already working on a plan for the good of
everyone. Please swap my anger with joy.*

Break the Chain

*Through him then let us continually offer up
a sacrifice of praise to God, that is, the fruit
of lips that acknowledge his name.*

HEBREWS 13:15 ESV

. . . .

Paul and Silas had simply wanted to set a possessed woman free. . .but instead ended up bound in chains themselves. Because of their intervention, her owners could no longer exploit her for money. And so Paul and Silas were beaten and then thrown in prison. The jailer fastened their feet and locked the cell doors.

As the night dragged on, Paul and Silas started to sing hymns of praise to God. Just then, an earthquake shook the very foundation of the prison. All the cell doors swung open and their chains broke apart.

Paul and Silas didn't praise God because they were happy about their imprisonment. They sang because God is worthy to be praised. The joy in their hearts—flowing from the awesomeness of the God they served—enabled them to be satisfied in this tragedy.

The chains that bind us today aren't literal chains. You can walk around thinking you're free, only to realize every door or window you see is locked. That's when it's time to praise—and then watch your chains break! True freedom is just around the corner!

. . . .

*Lord Jesus, I can't see a way out of this. But You are worthy
to be praised, and I thank You for being here with me in
the middle of my mess. My hope and joy are in You.*

Always

There is no fear in love. But perfect love drives out fear.
1 JOHN 4:18 NIV

. . . .

Tracy hung up the phone. She wanted to cry. This wasn't the first time it had happened, and she knew it probably wouldn't be the last. But still, it hurt tremendously. A rift had formed between her and someone she'd thought would be a lifetime friend. There was no official declaration, but she could see their friendship was nearing its end. Soon, they would be mere acquaintances—at best.

When a relationship implodes, it can immobilize you. It can stop you from wanting to connect with anyone new. It's difficult knowing that this person, whom you once felt close to, no longer wants anything to do with you. All the wonderful memories that come flooding back to you in that moment make it even more hurtful. And if you happen to be in a situation where you must continue seeing each other, it can be even harder.

The good news is that Jesus will *always* be there for you, without exception. He is in it for the long haul—for all eternity. God would never shun you if you became chronically sick—instead, He'd want to heal you. God will never bring up past offenses you've already confessed—instead, He's forgotten them.

Whatever issues you might have, Jesus is there for you—always!

. . . .

*God, thank You for understanding my hurts. I praise You
and rejoice in knowing You are always with me.*

A Long Way to Happy

Be happy in the Lord. And He will give you the
desires of your heart. Give your way over to the
Lord. Trust in Him also. And He will do it.
PSALM 37:4–5 NLV

Treasure maps, secret codes, hidden messages, rainbows—we've all heard that riches will follow each of these and bring us happiness. Many people pay a high price to try to find fulfillment through the "missing piece." They search everywhere to find what might fill the void in their lives, but instead, they lose most of themselves in the process. When they don't achieve their goals, their hearts are broken.

Earthly things can make you happy—temporarily, at least. There's an abundance of experiences and material things that can bring you pleasure, but they can also disappear or change in an instant. Through all your well-intended searching, lasting bliss seems to grow further and further out of reach.

However, when you serve God and praise Him, your desires will shift. You may *think* you need some flashy item, but what you *truly* need is to draw closer to God. Telling Him what you believe you want—and putting it in His hands—will produce better results that include real, lasting joy, not temporary happiness.

If the road to happiness appears long, that's because it is. Joy, however, is right around the corner.

God, thank You for fulfilling the desires of my heart. I won't continue
to search for happiness, but I will find joy in drawing closer to You.

What a Day!

This is the day that the LORD has made;
let us rejoice and be glad in it.

PSALM 118:24 ESV

Lillian woke up and turned off her alarm clock. It was too early, and she wasn't looking forward to her day. She made herself a cup of coffee, knowing it wouldn't change the way she was feeling. Between meetings, lunch, and college classes, she needed to get her vehicle checked out. It was going to be a rough day—she just knew it!

Victoria woke up to the smell of coffee. She found herself grateful yet again for the programmable coffeepot she'd been given. While she wasn't looking forward to her schedule that day, she was excited to meet some new people at her job. It was going to be a good day—she just knew it!

Attempting to put a positive spin on your day, especially when you don't see a reason to, can be a difficult task. Work, politics, relationship issues, health problems, and day-to-day responsibilities can leave you feeling overwhelmed. So it's imperative that you take notice of little things you're grateful for. . .and then tell God you're thankful.

When you focus on the bright side, the tone of your day will shift from dread to delight.

Father God, thank You for opening my eyes to all the little things I should be grateful for. I will rejoice in You and all my many blessings.

Check the Box

*Consider it pure joy, my brothers and sisters, whenever
you face trials of many kinds, because you know that
the testing of your faith produces perseverance.*
JAMES 1:2–3 NIV

• •

Alyssa felt like there was absolutely no way she could fulfill her God-given purpose. Between family drama, personal issues, and health battles, she was pretty sure that her God-given aspirations would never come to fruition. Anytime she seemed to be getting closer, something came along and derailed her progress.

The coffee on her desk was getting cold, and Alyssa was ready to give up for the day. The red pen that she used to check off boxes in her journal lay inside her desk drawer. It'd been months since she'd used it. She was sure that as soon as she started moving toward her goal, something would get in the way. But she was also certain she could persevere with God's help.

As long as you're breathing, you will consistently face obstacles. However, you can have pure joy despite those trials! That's because God can be trusted with the path He has for you. While it takes endurance to withstand life's tests, you can guarantee that God will follow through on His promises. And with that box checked off, the rest will fall into place.

• •

*God, I am so thankful that I can trust You,
regardless of what obstacles block my way.*

The Next Right Thing

Be happy in your hope. Do not give up when trouble comes.
ROMANS 12:12 NLV

- -

After losing their husbands, Naomi, Ruth, and Orpah had a decision to make concerning the rest of their lives. Naomi explained to her daughters-in-law that she would return to her people in Bethlehem. She encouraged them both to return to their hometowns. But Ruth chose to stay with Naomi. She told Naomi that she would follow wherever she went and that she would serve her God.

Even still, both women were grieving. Despite her bitterness and pain, Naomi devised a plan—and Ruth followed along. This plan led to Ruth finding favor with Boaz and eventually marrying him. Boaz, a man of wealth, restored their inheritance. And through his marriage to Ruth, the lineage of King David—and eventually Jesus—sprang forth.

Despite the devastation of their loss, Naomi and Ruth held on to hope. The misery they felt didn't keep them from taking action. They proceeded with what they knew to do, and they were blessed because of it.

When trouble comes, it's tempting to try to keep your life from changing. But when you act upon hope, the joy you receive could last for generations.

- -

Lord Jesus, though pain sometimes threatens to
paralyze me, I praise You for making my next steps
clear. I will act on the ideas You've given me.

New Car Smell

*"Until now you have not asked for anything in my name.
Ask and you will receive, and your joy will be complete."*

JOHN 16:24 NIV

. . . .

Chelsea lay awake, staring up at the ceiling. A long list of hopes and dreams ran unhindered through her mind. She wanted her bank account to be overflowing, her dream car parked in the driveway, and her house glistening with fine china and chandeliers. All of her prayers for these things had gone unanswered. And she was growing impatient.

It would be so convenient if all problems were fixed instantly. But the desire to have everything your way can turn your prayers into nothing more than wishes. As you pray, it can become nothing more than a long list of desires that you want addressed—*right now*! However, a true, heartfelt prayer seeks far more than material things.

When you pray in Jesus' name, it means He is signing off on the prayer. He can't sign off on things that clash with His kingdom. So while God may not sign off on your personal wish list, you can trust that His answers will bring a joy much greater than a new car smell.

. . . .

*Lord Jesus, I'm glad You want to hear everything on my heart.
Thank You for helping me be kingdom minded, which will
bring me greater joy than any material thing I think I need.*

Bridled

"Follow My teachings and learn from Me. I am gentle and do not have pride. You will have rest for your souls. For My way of carrying a load is easy and My load is not heavy."
MATTHEW 11:29–30 NLV

. . . .

A horse's bridle is intended to direct the horse the way it should go. The rider can easily guide the horse along the trails or mountainsides, keeping the horse from danger. But if the equipment isn't used properly, the rider could just as easily harm the horse.

Just like people who improperly use a bridle, many leaders, influencers, and authority figures misuse their platforms and end up hurting the people who look up to them. The act of following is not an easy task, and you've probably been failed by leaders you once looked up to.

People search many years—sometimes their whole lives—for guidance that will help make them whole. There are a ton of gurus and self-help writers out there, some of whom offer valuable information. But nothing in this world will leave you content like Jesus. When you follow Jesus, He promises rest for your soul. His commands aren't burdensome—they lead to freedom. And wherever freedom is, joy can flourish.

. . . .

God, I know Your plans for me lead to freedom and lasting joy. Thank You for guidance and discernment.

Don't Answer

For as high as the heavens are above the earth, so great is his love for those who fear him; as far as the east is from the west, so far has he removed our transgressions from us.

PSALM 103:11–12 NIV

. . . .

The covers on your bed are twisted from your perpetual tossing and turning. No matter how hard you try, you can't get comfortable. The little voice in your head keeps reminding you of every shameful moment in your life. You try to distract yourself with pleasant images and thoughts. But that little voice blabbers on, driving sleep further and further away.

Shame can invade your life and steal your peace, keeping you from experiencing joy. Regardless of whether you've confessed your sin to God and repented of it, the memory remains. And because you aren't equipped to forget your wrongs, regret can hover over you like an angry, black cloud.

Unlike you, God does have control over what He remembers. Whenever you confess your sin to God, He not only forgives, He forgets. He removes it from you as far as the east is from the west—an infinite distance.

So the next time shame comes knocking at your door, you don't have to answer.

. . . .

Father God, since You don't attach shame to me, I won't either. I will no longer let shame keep me from Your joy.

His Precious Creation

"Look at the birds. They don't plant or harvest or store food in barns, for your heavenly Father feeds them. And aren't you far more valuable to him than they are?"

MATTHEW 6:26 NLT

. . . .

Joelle turned off her car. Taking care of her mother was exhausting, and she wanted to sit there just a little while longer. There was no shortage of tasks that her mother needed assistance with—and Joelle helped with them all. Joelle walked inside the house with a hearty hello. Her mother smiled back, visibly relieved to see her. Instantly, she remembered why she was a caretaker. It was because of love.

Whether you are responsible for others' well-being or need assistance yourself, it's common to feel unseen. Regardless of your belief in God, you might still worry that your life isn't impacting anyone around you. But God knows the multitude of needs you have. He cares about each one, and He knows how to satisfy them.

Joy is hard to come by when you feel overlooked, but God looks on you with love and compassion as you go about your day. You are His most precious creation, and He will take care of your every need.

. . . .

God, I am so grateful for Your attention and love. Worry may try to overwhelm me, but I have joy because You see me.

Price Tag

There is no longer Jew or Gentile, slave or free,
male and female. For you are all one in Christ Jesus.
GALATIANS 3:28 NLT

. . . .

The invitations have been sent out, and the day of the celebration is near. All the phone calls have been made to verify time and location. Chefs are preparing the food for the expected number of people. There's no invitation in the mail for you, though. No food is being prepared for you to eat. The party doesn't include you. . .and you are devastated.

Ever since the invention of the school playground, there has been someone who's left out. If you were to list the reasons why anyone is excluded, you would eventually see a pattern—whatever the grounds may be, perceived differences can cause a lot of dissent.

While others may see you as inadequate, God does not. People in your life may want to leave you out of theirs, but God desires a relationship with you. Because of Jesus' sacrifice, God has no reason to leave you out of anything. In fact, it gives Him even more reason to include you. Many people miss out on relationships because they don't recognize their value. The price tag for a relationship between you and God was free for you—yet very costly to Him.

But He paid it in full.

. . . .

Father God, while I may feel excluded by others, I know I mean
a lot to You. Help me find joy in the truth of Your Word.

He Sees You

So the woman left her water jar and went away
into town and said to the people, "Come, see
a man who told me all that I ever did."

JOHN 4:28–29 ESV

. . . .

The idea of drawing water with all the other women did not appeal to her. They made her feel uncomfortable because she couldn't seem to find—or keep—a husband. So she decided to go alone. When she arrived, she saw a man standing at the well who asked her for water. She attempted to dismiss Him, but He continued to talk to her. As He validated her life experience, she accepted that He was the Christ and ran back to her village to share her joy. She forgot all about the water jar she had come to fill.

The Samaritan woman at the well didn't hesitate when she realized that she was known and loved—she left her water jar because it wasn't important anymore. What mattered was returning to the very people who had caused her pain—the people who were in pain themselves—and telling them of the man who had taken away her sorrow.

When you are overlooked or looked down upon, it can steal your happiness. Looking to others for approval will leave you wanting. But when you accept how God views you, your happiness will turn into even greater joy.

. . . .

Lord, I keep thinking about how I have been treated. Please
help me remember that Your opinion of me is all that matters.

Pity?

And if our hope in Christ is only for this life,
we are more to be pitied than anyone in the world.
1 CORINTHIANS 15:19 NLT

• •

Sometimes, you receive news that seems wrong on every level—and you know your life will never be the same. The struggle between having hope and dealing with reality weighs heavy on your soul. You feel like you have no choice but to live moment by moment and rely on support from the ones who love you.

At this moment, all over the globe, people are living out the consequences of our fallen world. When you watch the news and hear about the latest war—or when you have experienced great personal loss—it can be a stretch to believe in a good, loving God.

Even still, God *is* good. The Bible clearly teaches how to walk through trials—by looking directly at Jesus and His love for you. This life is not all there is, and Jesus has conquered this world. Someday, this constant, crippling pain will be forgotten.

When you place your hope in Christ Jesus, you can have lasting joy despite the tragedies. Pity just doesn't apply.

• •

Father God, while I don't have the answers,
I know You are working everything for my
good. I will continue to bless Your name.

Bricks

Those who sow in tears shall reap with shouts of joy! He who goes out weeping, bearing the seed for sowing, shall come home with shouts of joy, bringing his sheaves with him.

PSALM 126:5–6 ESV

. . . .

You've hit a brick wall. The time and work you've put into trying to make your vision come to life is conflicting with the reality of making it happen. While you believe with all your heart that your efforts will be worthwhile, all the signs are saying it is useless. Your heart drops.

Associating a smooth life with happiness is easy. It's wonderful when things go as planned without complications—when all your work is validated and you feel accomplished. But often, unforeseen problems come out of nowhere and wreck our expectations.

When God directs your steps, you may not know how the situation will end up. It's His job to control the outcome, and sometimes, it may not happen the way you'd hoped. Your job might be slightly more difficult—to believe over and over again, laying the bricks of faith. However, the intense joy that comes from seeing this brick wall morph into a building will be invaluable.

. . . .

Father God, I know You see my effort. Even though I don't know what to expect, I thank You for the perseverance that will lead to joy in Your name.

The End

"God blesses those who mourn,
for they will be comforted."
MATTHEW 5:4 NLT

• •

There are so many empty tissue boxes lying around that you wonder if you should've bought stock in the company. To make matters worse, this isn't the first time you've cried over this problem. You've prayed every way you know how. Nothing has changed.

Mourning can present itself in all sorts of different ways. Maybe instead of crying, you get angry or go completely numb. However you experience it, mourning is important. The last thing you need to do is to try masking what you feel to come across as superior. When you go to Jesus, He can bridge the gap where others may fall short.

Jesus never shied away from unwanted emotions, so neither should His people. When you walk with God through the pain, your relationship with Him grows stronger. You learn to spot all the ways He was with you in your grief, and in His comfort, you can find joy. Only after you accept the end of something can you get to the point where you can accept a new beginning. Endings are more important than you think—without them, nothing new could happen.

• •

Lord, I have a difficult time dealing with unwelcome emotions.
Thank You for not just consoling me but bringing solace too.

Work to Serve

Whatever you do, work at it with all your heart,
as working for the Lord, not for human masters.

COLOSSIANS 3:23 NIV

The wheels squeak on your office chair as you try to get comfortable. Your sweater was keeping you warm until you decided to take it off. Today might be the day that a fight breaks out between you and that coworker. Tensions have simmered for weeks, and you're just about to take the issue to the manager. One of you will have to go.

A hostile work environment can make it difficult to want to succeed. You've invested time and energy to get where you are. You've used all your resources in an attempt to find a solution. But at this moment of decision, it's imperative that you remember you aren't working only for other people. Someone may carry the title of boss, but that person isn't your *true* authority.

A work environment can become much simpler when you decide that you are working for the Lord. There is a bigger picture that stretches beyond your nine to five. That coworker that you can't seem to stand is someone whom your Father loves. When He says to love your enemies, it's because you'll find true joy in serving them.

God, my work environment is wearing on me. I will continue to
serve others because there is joy in following Your instructions.

Some Things Never Change

Jesus Christ is the same yesterday, today, and forever.
HEBREWS 13:8 NLT

. . . .

Going through your whole day feeling happy is unlikely to happen. Some annoyance will probably pop up. During your day, you may go from happy to excited to sad. Or maybe you started the day angry, and you only upgrade to slightly annoyed as the day progresses.

While humans have the ability to control their responses, nobody is immune to feeling a wide spectrum of emotions throughout the day. Even couples who are very much in love—and have been for years—will admit to not liking their partner from time to time. Emotions change quite frequently, and it can be difficult to deal with their ebb and flow.

When God says that He is constant, this means you never have to wonder about the way He views you. His love for you is assured. His actions toward you are pure. He has no hidden agendas. Other people in your life may keep you guessing about their true motives, but God does not. He wants to make His love for you abundantly clear. You can rest and take joy in the fact that you are known and loved—and *that* isn't going to change.

. . . .

Father God, I struggle with all the feelings that can come my way each day. I choose to find joy in Your steadfastness.

Left or Right?

"The Helper is the Holy Spirit. The Father will send Him in My place. He will teach you everything and help you remember everything I have told you."

JOHN 14:26 NLV

• •

Before there were maps to help people reach their destination, humanity looked to the stars. Now, a smooth, calm voice comes from your phone's GPS, gently telling you what direction to take. You want to comply, knowing that this computer knows the quickest route, but you also have to deal with backseat drivers.

There's no GPS to help you handle that individual who keeps insisting that this is, in fact, not the way you should go. The ones who say they know a better way rapidly erode your confidence, replacing it with fear and doubt.

It's possible to be a backseat driver when it comes to God's plan. That's why God sent the Holy Spirit—to empower you and establish your steps. The Holy Spirit moves alongside you to confirm the direction you should take. When you humble yourself and listen to His promptings, joy will follow you—whether you go left or right.

• •

Father God, I know I can't have joy in myself but only by dwelling in Your Spirit. Thank You for that joy that can only come through Your presence.

Like a Child

Jesus said, "Let the children come to me. Don't stop them! For the Kingdom of Heaven belongs to those who are like these children."

MATTHEW 19:14 NLT

. . . .

Lianne was exhausted. She had just spent her day at an event she had organized for the children in her church community. They had spent Sunday after Sunday telling her they wanted to do something fun, and after one child mentioned a water day, it was set. All the children immediately began helping Lianne plan what needed to be done. They spoke of nothing else.

It was a glorious day. She would never forget their faces as they slid down the waterslides and tossed water balloons. Or how the parents were walking around constantly taking pictures. Lianne smiled at all the children who came up and, with colorful grins from the snow cones they'd eaten, thanked her. While she may have organized it, it was the kids' passion and persistence that had really made it happen.

Children can be very determined when they want something. So when it comes to a relationship with God, He wants you to be like a child. The joy from pursuing Him is lifelong. Regardless of what may shift your happiness, your joy is rooted in a God who does not disappoint.

. . . .

Father God, I choose to pursue You the way a child would pursue something they desperately want. I know true satisfaction comes from You.

Winning

*For the kingdom of God is not a matter of
eating and drinking but of righteousness
and peace and joy in the Holy Spirit.*

Romans 14:17 esv

• •

Every game comes with a set of rules—it's no fun otherwise. If everyone interpreted the rules differently, chaos would ensue. Fights would break out over unfairness, and all the players would wonder what the real goal was.

It can be very easy to assume something that offends you must also offend others. You might immediately look down on someone for engaging in an activity you don't agree with. Any "good" person, you may say, wouldn't dare do such a thing!

Thankfully, the kingdom of heaven is not a game. It is relationship centered. There is no scale that measures you as better or worse than someone else. Instead, you are to take others into consideration and offer them peace and joy. Their reactions to the choices you make may seem confusing, but your ultimate goal should be unity. Whenever you genuinely get along with someone, despite different preferences or views, the joy that results is better than winning any game.

• •

*Lord Jesus, while I don't understand others' actions,
I know they are Your children. Thank You for helping
me reject division in favor of joyful love.*

Waiting

But they who wait upon the Lord will get new strength.
They will rise up with wings like eagles. They will run
and not get tired. They will walk and not become weak.

ISAIAH 40:31 NLV

- -

When sheep are out in the fields, they have to watch their shepherd. He tells them when it's safe to eat, drink, and rest. If they don't pay attention, they might get left behind. If they get too excited and try to run ahead of the shepherd, they'll still find themselves alone until he shows up.

Whenever you feel heavy and burdened, it might be because you have lost sight of Jesus. Jesus says that following Him is easy—that's because He is the one who's leading, not you. You were not meant to lead. You were intended to keep your focus on Jesus.

The sheep that stay with the shepherd, even though they may be impatient, are the most content. They may have to rest when they want to eat—or vice versa—but they have peace because the shepherd is guiding them. Their strength comes from his leadership.

There is joy in keeping pace with Jesus regardless of your desires. You might hate waiting, but you'll never have to wait alone.

- -

Father God, regardless of what I've set my heart on, I will wait
for You. My strength and joy aren't in myself but in You.

Expectation

*"But seek first the kingdom of God and his righteousness,
and all these things will be added to you."*
MATTHEW 6:33 ESV

Hannah sat alone in her room. The one thing she truly craved—the thing that would prove her worth and give her a sense of belonging—was to bear a child. Every passing month dragged her further and further from her heart's desire. She then promised God that if she had a son, he would remain in God's service all the days of his life.

Because Hannah sought God and His will for her, God answered her prayer. She birthed a son and named him Samuel. He would grow to be a prophet for God. But God didn't stop there: Hannah would go on to have five other children. The Lord didn't just give her what she asked—He fulfilled her dream unreservedly.

In that era, a woman's worth was attached to whether or not she could bear children. Today, you may not feel you need a child, but a whole host of other desires are tugging at your heart. Seek God. Go to Him first and lay your heart on the line. Let God replace your anxiety with joy—He'll go above and beyond what you expect.

*Lord Jesus, I know You see my heart. I trust You completely
with my dreams and know that You will fulfill me.*

Sucker Punch

*Then make me truly happy by agreeing wholeheartedly
with each other, loving one another, and working
together with one mind and purpose.*

PHILIPPIANS 2:2 NLT

• •

There's a reason that professional boxing is so popular. People don't spend money to see two men stand and stare at each other. They want to watch one man overtake the other. They want to cheer when one of the boxers is knocked out, despite the fact that violence is frowned upon in public.

In reality, whenever there is discord, an octagon doesn't materialize so that you can get inside and settle your differences. Conflicts require more civil solutions. This can be difficult when emotions are involved. It can be harder still if you want to avoid conflict at all costs.

When dissension arises, God calls for love—and one form of this love is humility. Showing restraint requires help from God. Fortunately, that's exactly what the Holy Spirit offers. When Paul wrote to the Philippians, he wanted to make it clear that when Christians prioritize love, working through differences together can be a joy.

Discord is not ideal—love is the ultimate sucker punch.

• •

*Lord Jesus, I'm surrounded by people who truly offend
me and make me want to lash out. Thank You for helping
me find what love looks like in these situations.*

Cracked

*My sacrifice, O God, is a broken spirit; a broken
and contrite heart you, God, will not despise.*
PSALM 51:17 NIV

- -

Adding a whole egg—shell and all—to a chocolate cake wouldn't make it taste very good. You have to break the egg for the recipe to work. Countless enjoyable dishes and desserts wouldn't exist if nobody cracked the eggs and mixed them properly with other ingredients.

Sometimes, you may feel so broken that Humpty Dumpty seems better off than you. No matter what encouragement others bring, you can't seem to hear it. Others may try to meet your needs, but their efforts fall flat. It's not that you're ungrateful—it's that you feel like you've shattered into a million pieces. Salvaging your crushed dreams looks impossible, but you just can't move on.

When you feel broken, that is the exact moment God can use you. You are not required to stay in your anguish—you just need to watch what He turns it into. Though sadness and anxiety may be pressing on every side, you can have joy in knowing that God never shies away from your emotions. What breaks God's heart is being out of relationship with you, so He'll welcome you however you may come to Him—cracks and all.

- -

*Father God, I come before You exactly as I am. I know that You love
me. . .and that Your love for me won't leave me the way I came.*

Mine

*Rejoice always, pray without ceasing, give
thanks in all circumstances; for this is the
will of God in Christ Jesus for you.*
1 THESSALONIANS 5:16–18 ESV

From minerals to metals, there are a vast number of assets that are mined. Miners sift through tons of dirt and clay to obtain these materials from the earth.

The Bible instructs us to pray, rejoice, and give thanks without ceasing. This means that in any situation, it's possible to mine thankfulness and praise. Sounds like a tall order, right? After all, reality often isn't conducive to those things. Many events seem to conspire each day to hinder your ability to walk in thankfulness and praise.

Paul, who wrote Thessalonians, spent quite a bit of his ministry in jail. But he didn't let this stop or hinder his love for Christ or His people. Because he found reasons to be thankful and praise God behind bars, Paul was able to write roughly half of the New Testament. Regardless of what you have to face, God enables you to have joy while praising Him. It may seem harder than mining for gold, but when you do, you can say, "Thankfulness and joy are mine!"

*Lord Jesus, while I may not easily find thankfulness or be
able to rejoice in any situation, I know it's possible. Thank
You for opening my eyes so that I can be closer to You.*

Second Opinion

But the wisdom from above is first pure, then peaceable, gentle, open to reason, full of mercy and good fruits, impartial and sincere.

JAMES 3:17 ESV

· ·

Doctors and surgeons spend years in school studying how to help their patients. They are required to meet situations with realistic expectations, not ones based in fantasy. Whenever emotions are involved, outcomes become unclear. In health care, remaining levelheaded is key.

Imagine having a serious illness. . .and your doctor just smiles and says everything will be fine. Despite how you feel, he simply dismisses you. Everything is obviously not fine, but the doctor keeps assuring you that it is.

It is easy to do the same thing to yourself—to stand by and convince yourself that everything is fine. But covering up or glossing over issues doesn't lead to a solution. With wisdom, however, problems can be addressed fully. Wisdom allows you to be not okay while still having hope and joy. God understands reality, but He has a way of making it fantastic. The next time your brain tries to make less of a situation, go to God for a second opinion.

· ·

Father God, I know that with Your help, I can face this circumstance head-on. I ask for Your pure, peaceable wisdom. Thank You for producing joy from life's pain.

Following

"The Lord your God is with you, a Powerful One Who wins the battle. He will have much joy over you. With His love He will give you new life. He will have joy over you with loud singing."

ZEPHANIAH 3:17 NLV

. . . .

The phrase "following God" is a common term in Christianity. "Following" someone can imply that you are behind—that you're doing your best but will never quite catch up. This can make you feel like you are not enough.

When you are in a relationship with God, He is right next to you. Whatever you might be fighting, He will win your battle. When you give your struggles to God, that's when they can be defeated.

God also takes great delight in you. He doesn't frown or glare down at you; rather, He's glad He made you. God *never* regrets the price He paid for you. Because of His love for you, He sent His Son, Jesus, so that you could have a new and better life.

The best part is that just as you rejoice in the Lord, He rejoices over you. It's not one-sided. You aren't following someone who doesn't care. You're following a God who cheers you on.

. . . .

Lord, I fully submit to Your leadership. I know that in doing so, I will gain love and joy like I've never known before.

Time Travel

"Forget the former things; do not dwell on the past. See, I am doing a new thing! Now it springs up; do you not perceive it? I am making a way in the wilderness and streams in the wasteland."

ISAIAH 43:18–19 NIV

The sun was shining, the colors seemed more vibrant, and Monica just knew it was going to be a lovely day. She decided to go outside and read a book on her patio. But as soon as she opened the door, the smell of the flowers opened the floodgates of memory. Stunned, she wanted to curl up on the floor. She remembered everything, down to what everyone was wearing. It wasn't a moment she cared to relive.

Whenever you try to move on from something, memory can be your worst enemy. It can keep you trapped in a time and place you desperately want to leave. And as long as you're paralyzed like this, no progress can be made.

Thankfully, you serve a God who works in the present. There's no need to dwell on the past—God isn't there. He is doing a new thing for you right now. Instead of time traveling to a heartbreaking past, focus on the joy God has for you in the present.

Lord, I sometimes relive my past, not even by choice. I choose today to leave it behind and look for the good You have for me.

47

Words

Out of the same mouth come praise and cursing.
My brothers and sisters, this should not be. Can both
fresh water and salt water flow from the same spring?
JAMES 3:10–11 NIV

- -

An old adage says "Sticks and stones may break my bones but words will never hurt me." Science would beg to differ. There are countless experiments that prove that words—positive or negative—can affect you and your surroundings.

Your initial reaction when presented with an obstacle is natural. However, what you say can have a huge impact on how the situation plays out. Speaking positively about a situation isn't ignoring reality— it's helping to create a new one. If you can accept how you feel about a problem but choose to speak life over it anyway, the solution might become clearer.

God used His words to create the world. You are created in His image, so the words you speak show what you are partnering with. It might be tempting to allow your feelings to dictate your words, but that can keep you stuck where you are. Despite the reality that's right in front of your face, God wants you to join Him in creating a better one.

- -

Lord, You and I both know the gravity of my
problem. I choose to speak constructively and know
that You're making a way for me regardless.

Worthwhile

*"For sure, I tell you, you will cry and have sorrow,
but the world will have joy. You will have
sorrow, but your sorrow will turn into joy."*

JOHN 16:20 NLV

Life was going quite well for Jessica. . .until it wasn't. She had a good support group, but even they couldn't drown out the crowd reveling in her misfortune. Still, Jessica knew her decision was right. It was better to go back to the drawing board now rather than later. Jessica had done the difficult thing, and all she could do was hope it would be worthwhile.

Doing the right thing can be grueling. Jesus, who gave His life for yours, knows that all too well. When He was preparing His disciples for His death, He warned them of the sorrow that it would bring them. Jesus explained that many people would rejoice during His crucifixion, but He also made sure they knew it wouldn't end that way.

Sometimes, it can appear that your walk with the Lord will lead to utter devastation. It can seem like what you love will give way to despair and agony. It won't. While you don't know the ending, God does—and He guarantees it will be worthwhile.

*God, things don't look good for me. I surrender this
all to You, knowing You will use this for Your glory.
I trust You will turn my sorrow into joy.*

Everything?

For I can do everything through Christ,
who gives me strength.
PHILIPPIANS 4:13 NLT

Today's Bible verse is very popular—you can find it on anything from shirts to bumper stickers. It is preached from the pulpits as a reminder that all things are possible with God. It's used to remind you that with Him, you can overcome any obstacle. But is that true?

Paul the apostle was speaking about how, regardless of what state he found himself in, he was content in Christ. He wanted nothing more than to be in God's will, and he had faith that God would honor that. Paul never questioned why he found himself in a situation. He determined that no matter what trial he faced, God would walk him through it.

At one point or another, you will face something that makes it painfully obvious that you need God. At that moment, it's important to ask yourself if you've missed the directions God has for your life. That can cause lots of pain and remove any chance of obtaining real joy. God gives you strength to do everything He needs you to do. So while you can't do everything you want and expect God to give you strength, you can have joy in His strength when you are in His will.

Father God, I want to follow the path You have for me. While that
isn't always clear, I know You'll give me the strength to do it.

Lasting Results

And this world is fading away, along with
everything that people crave. But anyone who
does what pleases God will live forever.

1 JOHN 2:17 NLT

. . . .

You've seen the advertisements everywhere, even this morning on television. A lot of your friends on social media have been gushing about it as well. Upon hitting "buy," you immediately feel a rush of excitement. Once the product arrives, your happiness turns to hopelessness as the sobering truth sets in: *I've been scammed.*

We're all looking for a quick fix for our problems. That pill, lotion, or potion that will finally solve everything. From physical appearance to mental capacity, each improvement you think you need has a product designed for it. Unfortunately, because it is of this world, results may vary.

This world isn't going to last forever, so the happiness it provides will be fleeting. But with God, you don't have to wonder if you've been scammed. He is who He says He is, and He does what He says He will. If you put your trust in the Lord, your happiness will be replaced with joy, not hopelessness. When you please God, you get lasting results.

. . . .

Father God, I give my undesirable circumstances to You. I will
put my trust in You and not in the things of this world.

Follow the Son

For the moment all discipline seems painful rather than pleasant, but later it yields the peaceful fruit of righteousness to those who have been trained by it.

HEBREWS 12:11 ESV

Sunflowers not only look like the sun—they follow the sun during the day. From dawn until dusk, the sunflowers watch the sun on its journey from east to west. Once the day is done, the sunflower closes up, waiting for the next opportunity to revel in the sun's nurturing presence.

Just like the sunflower, people naturally gravitate toward what makes them happy. When trouble or adversity comes—and the option to sin is appealing—it's tempting to shut down and wonder where God is or if He even cares. It can also seem as if you are being taught a lesson, since happiness has left you alone.

When you are choosing to do what is right, you may experience distressing degrees of loss. No type of suffering seems joyous while you are in the middle of it. But if you choose to forgo temporary happiness, you'll gain peace in following the Holy Spirit. It is in your darkest affliction that you can experience the brightest joys because God is your sustenance and source of delight.

God, I want to be the flower that doesn't close up when the sun goes away. Thank You for letting me bask in Your glory and joy, no matter what.

Where Do You Live?

Honor and majesty surround him;
strength and joy fill his dwelling.
1 CHRONICLES 16:27 NLT

. . . .

He heard his father coming, and he knew what he would say. His father would tell him they had no choice but to celebrate his younger brother's return. While he understood they should be happy that his little brother was back, he never would've guessed the celebration would be this big.

He'd watched the day his brother left. . .and how it broke his father's heart. But the older brother had stayed, willing to serve and obey his father. Yet nobody ever threw a party like this for *him*. He couldn't help but feel a little jilted. Why? Because he had forgotten that he lives in the place where the celebrations happen.

Later in the story, the father reminds the older son that all the father has is his. In this life, it's important that you remember you have access to the Holy Spirit every moment. At any point, you have the ability to dwell in God's majesty, strength, and joy. No special accommodations are needed—it is yours because you are His child. Whenever you feel you are not getting the recognition you deserve, you need to remind yourself whose house you dwell in.

. . . .

Lord Jesus, as Your child, I know that all that You have is mine. I am
so grateful that Your love, joy, peace, and strength are there for me.

Rest Easy

*And we know that in all things God works
for the good of those who love him, who have
been called according to his purpose.*

ROMANS 8:28 NIV

. . . .

Amanda crumpled the bill in her hand. She was upset. She had been working so hard, but it didn't seem like it was enough. This feeling was becoming all too familiar. She didn't know how she kept finding herself in this situation. She'd worked as hard as she possibly could. *I've exhausted all options,* she thought to herself. Then Amanda smiled. *I've exhausted all my options. . .which means that God will have to show up.* Her experience with Him was that He was always right on time.

All things. Those are two very broad words. To think of a scenario or circumstance that isn't covered by them is impossible—just as God intended. God works all things together for your good. He only requires that you love and serve Him.

There will be times where there will be nothing else you can do but relieve a situation. It is in those moments you can let peace wash over you. Because until you come across a predicament that doesn't fall under the category of "all things," you can rest easy.

. . . .

*God, You're the only solution to this problem. I am so grateful for
that. I will have joy while waiting to see what You will do.*

Autopilot

*For God is working in you, giving you the desire
and the power to do what pleases him.*
PHILIPPIANS 2:13 NLT

The temperature outside was perfect, so Sabrina decided to travel home from work with her windows down. This was one day she didn't mind the somewhat lengthy drive. The miles flew by as if she were on autopilot, and before she knew it, she was home. *If only life could go that smoothly,* she thought.

When you think about doing good works, it's easy to dwell on the rewards and recognition that might result. This, however, can lead to emptiness—God will not share His glory with you. Whatever praise you may get will fall flat because it does not truly belong to you.

Only by faith can you do good works. To demonstrate faith, you must do what God has prepared for you to do—abide in Christ and walk in Spirit and in truth. When you do, your joy will be complete because all the glory will go to Him.

When God moves through you, it's easier than using autopilot.

*Lord, please direct all my steps in a way that gives You glory.
Any joy I have over a good deed is for You and because of You.*

Pick-Me-Up

*How we thank God for you! Because of you we
have great joy as we enter God's presence.*
1 THESSALONIANS 3:9 NLT

. . . .

"Amen," she said as she got up off the floor. Sharissa was determined to pray for her friend every day. When she prayed, the Holy Spirit guided her words, and each time it was different. Sharissa heard her phone ring and answered it. She couldn't help but laugh and praise God as she listened to her friend recount all the wonderful things that had happened for her.

Regular daily living can bombard you with so many problems that it can be hard to focus on anyone but yourself. It's a struggle to function in your own world—much less to be concerned with anyone else's. When you are at a low point yourself, it can be hard to raise others up.

When Paul wrote today's verse to the Thessalonians, he was explaining how his joy was full because his prayers for them had been answered. He had been writing to them and praying for them—all from a jail cell. Paul still had great joy because God had heard and answered his prayer for others. So if you are feeling down and need a pick-me-up, lift up others in prayer.

. . . .

*Father God, help me focus more on others and how to pray for
them. I look forward to completing our joy as Your will is fulfilled.*

Deep Roots

*Who is a God like you, who pardons sin and forgives
the transgression of the remnant of his inheritance?
You do not stay angry forever but delight to show mercy.*
MICAH 7:18 NIV

Trees must be embedded deep in the ground in order for them to flourish. If they aren't firmly planted, a strong gust of wind may topple them over, causing substantial damage to anything nearby. But the trees whose roots go deep are unfazed by anything nature throws at them.

All joy has its roots in love. How much joy something gives you can be measured by how much love you have for it. Joy is the highest declaration that can be given to your enjoyment of something. So the more you love, the greater your joy will be.

When you turn from your sin and ask God to forgive you, you increase not only your own joy but His. His mercy directly reflects how deep His love is for you. Regardless of what you have done, you don't have to wonder if you are loved. His mercy runs deep. When you are rooted in that love, nothing will be able to faze you.

*Lord Jesus, thank You for Your mercy that shows just
how much You love me. Just as You delight in my
redemption, I will praise You for my salvation.*

Never Gonna Say Goodbye

"All right then, the Lord himself will give you the sign. Look! The virgin will conceive a child! She will give birth to a son and will call him Immanuel (which means 'God is with us')."

ISAIAH 7:14 NLT

- -

Saying goodbye is hard—it can be even harder when you don't get the chance to. There are things we think will never change. . .but they do. It can be heartbreaking to depend on something, only for it to disappear. Abandonment is labeled as trauma for a reason.

Sometimes, people make decisions based solely on their fear of being alone. They go to great lengths to ensure they are included in whatever activity may be going on. Their social life brings them happiness, so when it is taken away, they are gripped with anguish.

To have joy, your heart has to open and welcome what it desires. For that to happen, the message your heart receives has to be good. There's no better message than that of Jesus Christ. No other good news can measure up, and no bad news can replace it. Immanuel means "God with us." With God, you never have to say goodbye.

- -

Father God, I hate having to say goodbye to what I know. Thank You for always being with me and surrounding me with Your love, even when I can't feel it.

Dying to Live

"For whoever wants to save their life will lose it,
but whoever loses their life for me will find it."
MATTHEW 16:25 NIV

. . . .

Regardless of your culinary preferences, whatever is on your plate is no longer living. The thing that gave it life is gone. It is now giving you energy—and with it, the ability to live.

It is counterintuitive to not do everything in your power to maximize your comfort. Inconvenience never brings anyone great joy. The idea of serving someone is not generally one's first thought upon waking.

When Jesus told His disciples that they would have to die in order to live, they were confused. It didn't seem natural. That's because it isn't—it's spiritual. You are never more like Jesus than when you're giving up your life for others.

The idea that death makes room for life is exemplified over and over again throughout God's creation. When you set aside your needs and desires for those around you, you are picking up your cross and following Jesus. There is immeasurable joy to be found in that kind of dying.

. . . .

God, I want to be a vessel for You. I willingly lay down my
convenience to make room for the joyful life You have for me.

The Table Is Set

You prepare a table before me in the presence of my enemies; you anoint my head with oil; my cup overflows.

PSALM 23:5 ESV

. . . .

The Bible uses the dynamic between a shepherd and his sheep to illustrate the relationship between God and His children. A shepherd would put oil on his flock's heads to protect them from harmful, disease-spreading bugs. And when it came time for the sheep to eat, the shepherd would guide them to where they needed to go. Even if predators were nearby, the sheep listened to the shepherd and ate without worry.

Wherever relationships are involved, worry is as well. The line between friend and enemy sometimes wears thin. One moment, you are the best of friends; the next moment, you are astounded at their audacity and the relationship devolves. And that's not counting the people whom you don't immediately mesh with and can only handle in smaller doses.

It can be hard to believe that you are in God's will whenever you are surrounded by difficult and unlovable people. But because the sheep were guarded by their shepherd, they ate in peace. No matter whom you find yourself eating with, you can rejoice knowing it is God who set the table.

. . . .

At times, Lord, I can feel like I have many enemies. Thank You for putting me where I'm supposed to be and for being my source of peace and joy.

Nothing but the Truth

For I am not ashamed of this Good News about Christ.
It is the power of God at work, saving everyone
who believes—the Jew first and also the Gentile.
ROMANS 1:16 NLT

The telephone game has been around for quite a while. The fun comes from the fact that the phrase you start the game with is usually completely different by the time the last player yells it out. Everyone laughs at the new, distorted phrase's absurdity.

This game is a great illustration of how gossip can spiral out of control. Before anyone knows it, multiple people are hurt. Even with news and social media readily available, getting all the facts seems harder than ever. You can be left wondering what the truth is, which can make you feel helpless.

When you share the news of Jesus, you don't have to be concerned that it might hurt or tarnish someone. You can have joy knowing that your act of sharing the gospel has the ability to turn a person's life around completely. If you don't know the exact words, just follow the promptings of the Holy Spirit. The truth has a way of changing lives for the better, and the good news of Jesus Christ is for everyone.

Lord Jesus, thank You for giving me the boldness to spread the news
of Your love. I have such joy knowing Your love is trustworthy.

DNA Test

For we are God's masterpiece. He has created
us anew in Christ Jesus, so we can do the
good things he planned for us long ago.
EPHESIANS 2:10 NLT

Marketing companies wouldn't make much money if all people thought they were perfect. Companies count on the fact that when you look in the mirror, you see flaws and want to fix them. Whatever you believe you need, you'll end up sparing no expense to get them.

It's one thing to perceive a flaw and try to change it—it's another thing entirely to feel like you are less than because of that flaw. Instead of looking in the mirror and thinking you need to fix your hair or change your lipstick, you only see how your DNA is wrong.

God created you. Whatever you see in the mirror is right. You are correct in how you look. There's no need to feel miserable about the things you can't change about yourself. Instead, let God change your mind.

Let Him show you the joy you were made for—that is something a DNA test can't tell you.

Father God, I feel bombarded with others' opinions
of how I should look. Thank You for healing my
mind and helping me ignore these pressures.

The Winner Is. . .

*And whatever you do or say, do it as a representative of the
Lord Jesus, giving thanks through him to God the Father.*
COLOSSIANS 3:17 NLT

Millions of people tune in to the Olympics, watching in fascination as
athletes push their bodies to the limit. During the commercials, viewers
wonder how incredible it would be to have such a flexible, resilient
body. Everyone claps as the winner is given the gold medal—there's
no jealousy, just cheers in celebration.

Everyday life is much different. Whenever you see your friend's
brand-new car or that expensive house down the street, envy wells up
within you. Your feelings of entitlement take residence in your brain,
making you feel dissatisfied with the life you've always known.

Entitlement can make you feel like you deserve everything you don't
have. Gratitude, however, causes you to thank the Lord for everything
He has given you. Whenever you remember whom you serve—and
all the ways He takes care of you—thankfulness comes naturally. That
thankfulness removes jealousy and makes way for joy. While you may
not get a golden medal, you will no longer feel second rate.

*Father God, instead of thinking about what I want,
I want to thank You for what I do have. I am Your
child, and I want Your glory to be known.*

Start to Finish

I am sure that God Who began the good work
in you will keep on working in you until
the day Jesus Christ comes again.
PHILIPPIANS 1:6 NLV

• •

Anna sat down, staring hopelessly at her to-do list. Somehow, she'd grossly overestimated how much she could get done in a day. *Who did I think I was?* she thought. *A superhero?* Not everything would get done, and that really irked her.

The ability to follow through on a project is a valuable trait. The occasional incomplete jigsaw puzzle is frustrating enough, but to leave a to-do list consistently undone can compound your feelings of failure. What was once a manageable situation soon becomes overwhelming.

Unlike you, God *can't* leave something half-finished. What God starts, He completes. When you look at yourself, you may see all the imperfections and unfinished work, but God sees Jesus. This is meant not as an excuse to sin but as a reminder that when you do sin, you can have joy instead of shame. You can rejoice that the God you serve will be with you from start to finish.

• •

Father God, there's a lot in my life that needs to be fixed.
Thank You for making me whole with Your love.

Perfecting Peace

"Peace I leave with you. My peace I give to you. I do not give peace to you as the world gives. Do not let your hearts be troubled or afraid."

JOHN 14:27 NLV

. . . .

Angela liked to have everything in order—it made her feel more in control. When she got to work, she realized that Genine hadn't finished her part of the project. Apparently, she could not rely on her coworkers. She wanted to scream, but she kept her composure. Next time, she'd do it by herself.

Whenever you want things to be just right, the smallest inconvenience can become intolerable. It takes great effort to continuously perform at such a high level. When you take on so many obligations, it can feel like the weight of the world is on your shoulders. When you desire perfection, you start noticing corruption everywhere.

Nothing in this life will ever be perfect—you must learn to rejoice through imperfection. You can only feel what you have the capacity for, however; that's why God sent you the Holy Spirit—so that you can have true peace among discord. Let His peace perfect you, and you'll find joy in the midst of chaos.

. . . .

Lord, I hate dealing with a mess that's out of my control. I hand this over to You, because I know You won't let me down.

Helping God

"And the very hairs on your head are all numbered.
So don't be afraid; you are more valuable to
God than a whole flock of sparrows."
LUKE 12:7 NLT

Bethany enjoyed helping people out—she was thrilled every time she saw someone's needs met. Sometimes, however, assisting others got under her skin. Anytime she was overlooked or taken advantage of, she began feeling unloved. Being a leader was very easy—what was not easy was going unrecognized for her hard work. Bethany realized she may need to learn how to say no.

Determining your worth from the validation others give you is dangerous. It can leave you feeling empty and unseen. Being empathetic and meeting people's needs is admirable, but it could make you feel like you need to protect yourself from the constant demands of others. You have needs as well, and resentment can rise up if they are not met.

You don't have to wonder what God needs, because His love for you has made that clear. He wants nothing from you. . .except *you*! He knows every hair on your head. You are valuable to Him. Your joy isn't in helping God but in finding Him valuable in return. God doesn't need your help—He wants love, specifically from you.

Father God, serving others can leave me exhausted. I will remember
the value I have in You and let Your love flow through me to others.

Achieving Dreams

For by grace you have been saved through faith.
And this is not your own doing; it is the gift of God,
not a result of works, so that no one may boast.
EPHESIANS 2:8–9 ESV

Camille was all dressed and ready to go for the awards ceremony. After all she'd accomplished, she was finally in the running to win an award. The dinner and desserts were quickly eaten, and now came the moment of truth. Camille's name was never called—she lost out to her colleague. Her clapping was as empty as she felt.

When your best is not enough—when you're unable to get the status you crave—you might start feeling like less of a person. You may appear like you have it all together, but you're still terrified that others will look down on you. You've met all the demands that others have put on you, yet you still feel as if you fall short.

God's love for you is not tied to what you do. There's no need to strive when you are in His presence. Spend your energy on being with God. Joy isn't in what you do but in the one for whom you do it. Achieving your dreams is wonderful, but hearing God say "well done" is better.

God, I recognize that any glory my success brings belongs to You.
I will find joy in Your love when I feel like I'm not enough.

Individual Pieces

But in fact God has placed the parts in the body,
every one of them, just as he wanted them to be.
If they were all one part, where would the body be?
1 Corinthians 12:18–19 NIV

Clea felt like something was missing. Everyone around her seemed to have it all together. . .but not her. Inside, she felt like a puzzle with a missing piece—a piece that had slid under the floorboards, never to be found. Clea didn't want to be ordinary, and she was jealous of others who seemed comfortable in their own skin.

When you want to be unique, normal appears frightening. You spend so much time trying to stand out that you don't realize you're alienating others. You have the capacity to help others in pain, but you don't feel whole enough to do so. When you feel so different, the life of a hermit seems more and more appealing.

Since God made you, nothing is missing. Your feelings may scream that you are defective, but that's a lie. If everyone were exactly the same, life would be very boring. You can find joy in your uniqueness because God fashioned it. You may feel like scattered puzzle pieces, but God sees the whole picture each individual piece can make.

Father God, feeling different is frustrating. I praise You
that I am missing nothing and that I am whole in You.

Investigating God

God did this so that, by two unchangeable things in which it is impossible for God to lie, we who have fled to take hold of the hope set before us may be greatly encouraged.
HEBREWS 6:18 NIV

. . . .

Julianne's observation was that most people were just too confident. There were too many factors involved in any given subject. She didn't feel comfortable until she knew all the facts. When it came to herself, however, she felt like *that* was a subject she'd never understand. Julianne would stick to the intellectual side of things. That was safer.

The desire to be alone and organize your thoughts is a strong one. The world inside your head can be much more manageable than the real one. Everything makes sense there, and you have the facts to back everything up. It can also be baffling when others don't put the same amount of thought into issues as you do.

True knowledge and understanding can be found in a relationship with God because He cannot lie. When you let go of what you think you know, you'll be able to rejoice in the hope He has given you. God's pure love for you may not make sense, but it's definitely worth the investigation.

. . . .

Father God, I will seek out the knowledge and wisdom that comes from You. Your steadfast love for me is my joy.

Where's the Loyalty?

*And this same God who takes care of me will
supply all your needs from his glorious riches,
which have been given to us in Christ Jesus.*

PHILIPPIANS 4:19 NLT

Minnie was concerned. Every time she looked on social media or watched the news, she saw that something awful was headed her way. She had to protect all her loved ones. Her mind was plagued by all the uncertainty. No one else seemed to share Minnie's worry—and that's what irritated her the most. She would just have to continue to search for what would help her prepare.

When no one appears to take you seriously, it can be hard to relax. You spend so much of your time preparing for what could happen that you can miss what is happening. It's difficult to know whom to trust when you doubt the confidence you see in others. You just know that you have to handle situations perfectly, or else others might not return the love you have for them.

Thankfully, God sees every facet of any situation. The Bible says God supplies not some but *all* of your needs. He sent the Holy Spirit to guide you through any uncertainty. The rest and joy you crave is found in God's loyalty and love toward you.

*God, I see trouble all around me. I will trust Your Holy Spirit
to guide me because I know You take care of Your children.*

Enthusiastically Brave

Satisfy us each morning with your unfailing love,
so we may sing for joy to the end of our lives.
PSALM 90:14 NLT

. . . .

Everyone considered Bernadette the life of any party. She could carry on an animated conversation about practically any topic. But while Bernadette loved to have fun, she sometimes felt a little hollow. Still, it was easier to move on to the next fun thing than to deal with her own emotions. As long as she wasn't bored, she could manage.

Facing reality can be difficult. When there are so many fun experiences to be had, dealing with negativity and pain can be an afterthought. Since others expect you to make them happy, you can start feeling burnt out quickly. Soon, all that "fun" becomes little more than a cage.

With God, however, you can not only face reality but rejoice in it. You don't need to cower away from what's going on around— or inside—you. Your satisfaction and completion can be found each day in the love God has for you. You may wish to neglect the present, but God's love can make you enthusiastically brave.

. . . .

Lord Jesus, finding happiness is important to me, but I know
it pales in comparison to the joy that's found in Your love.

Challenge Accepted

"The LORD will fight for you; you need only to be still."
EXODUS 14:14 NIV

. . . .

Sophia couldn't stand people being treated badly, especially those she loved. The next time it happened, she knew exactly what to do. She'd simply confront the people involved, explaining to them how they could have handled themselves better. She was trying her best to control her temper. . .but it seemed more and more like a losing battle.

When you have control over a situation, you feel powerful. You don't have to worry about being humiliated—you are in charge. The last thing you want to witness (or experience) is injustice. The idea of standing by while any form of abuse happens is appalling.

Like any good soldier, you must realize that you can't fight every battle by yourself. When you join with the Holy Spirit and give the fight to God, it changes the battleground. Deciding to pray instead of attacking makes room for God to move. The Lord will fight for you. You don't have to feel vulnerable—you can rejoice over what God will do. Being still in the presence of God isn't always easy, but it's a challenge worth accepting.

. . . .

God, whenever I want to handle a situation all by myself, remind me of the joy that will come when I let You take the wheel.

Realizing Peace

For to set the mind on the flesh is death, but to
set the mind on the Spirit is life and peace.
ROMANS 8:6 ESV

• •

Aimee was most satisfied when life went smoothly. She thrived on predictability and stability. In general, she was very easygoing, but when anything interrupted her plans, it really threw her off. Any confrontation made her want to give up. Aimee knew it was unrealistic for everything to be perfect all the time, but it was just easier to space out.

When you want harmony, even small interruptions can trip you up. It's easy to be agreeable and go with the flow. . .until something comes along that raises your stress level. Then you become indecisive, paralyzed, stagnant. Resigning yourself to stay put until the disruption is gone may lead to losing yourself in the process.

You can't always be insulated from discord. When you have constant communion with the Holy Spirit, He enables you to walk along the path of true peace. This is far better than the contentment and harmony you've created for yourself. There is joy in placing your need for serenity in the hands of God—only then can you realize true peace.

• •

Father God, I feel like I lose myself a little each time I am faced with
conflict. Thank You for giving me Your indestructible joy and peace.

Intrusive Mercy

Though formerly I was a blasphemer, persecutor,
and insolent opponent. But I received mercy
because I had acted ignorantly in unbelief.
1 TIMOTHY 1:13 ESV

Imagine if none of us kept our thoughts and feelings to ourselves. Optimistic thoughts wouldn't pose any problems; it's the self-deprecating thoughts that would cause much of the pain. They'd make you feel sad and disappointed, especially if that's not who you are anymore.

You are a witness to everything you think and feel. When you are bombarded with intrusive thoughts, you may feel ashamed or perhaps even worthless. They make you wonder if what you've done in your past has stolen your value in the present.

There is a reason that God makes it clear in His Word that you have forgiveness in Jesus Christ. Realizing the magnitude of your sin can be devastating, but if you've confessed, Jesus has already forgotten it! These thoughts don't have to rule you or steal your joy. Let God's mercy determine your worth. His mercy outweighs any intrusive thoughts.

Father God, I feel so bad about the things I've done.
Some I was aware of—others I was not. Thank You for
Your mercy and grace, which silence my shame.

Learn Your Blessings

But if you look carefully into the perfect law that sets
you free, and if you do what it says and don't forget
what you heard, then God will bless you for doing it.
JAMES 1:25 NLT

· ·

When you were in school, remember how often you crammed for a test? The night before, you would spend a ton of time going over all the material, just hoping you'd remember it the next day. Most of the time, that worked, and you'd end up passing the test. However, how much of that information do you recall now?

Having all the information on a subject is great. The confidence it can bring you is immeasurable. Any question that is asked, you can answer it because you're prepared. But if you can't remember this information, what's the use? It doesn't matter how much you know—it's the things you don't know that can cause difficulties.

Many people are unhappy because they are bound by what they don't know. God's Word tells you there is freedom in Jesus Christ. If you find yourself joyless, it might be because you are lacking knowledge of Him and the freedom that it brings. When you learn more about God, He blesses you for it.

· ·

Father God, I want to learn more about who You are. Thank You for
Your mercy and grace through Jesus that allow me to do just that.

75

Who Hurt You?

Let us then with confidence draw near to the throne of grace, that we may receive mercy and find grace to help in time of need.

HEBREWS 4:16 ESV

. . . .

Wild porcupines are not the friendliest of creatures. They don't like any strange creatures coming near them. Lots of dogs, thinking a porcupine might be a friend, have been found later with a face full of quills. After a trip to the vet, the dog may wonder who could have possibly hurt the porcupine that much.

Your life experiences can make it hard to relate to people, let alone the Creator and Master of the universe. The idea of opening up and sharing a piece of your soul is frightening. When you are used to people letting you down, it can be hard to believe that God is any different.

As uncomfortable as it might be, God wants you to come boldly before Him. You might have a long list of reasons for why you don't feel adequate enough to present yourself to God, but you can throw that away. When you have the confidence that God's grace and mercy give you, joy will take the place of fear. No one will be asking, "Who hurt you?"

. . . .

Father God, as timid as I may feel talking with You, I know Your love for me means I can be bold. Thank You for replacing my apprehension with the joy that comes from a relationship with You.

Unavailable Bright Side

*Not only that, but we rejoice in our sufferings, knowing
that suffering produces endurance, and endurance
produces character, and character produces hope.*

ROMANS 5:3–4 ESV

. . . .

The human body is very adaptable when it comes to withstanding harsh weather and pain. Science shows that it takes roughly two weeks of spending time outdoors before one becomes "outdoor acclimatized." Similarly, you may walk around awhile, squinting and rubbing your eyes, before you realize you have a headache.

It isn't always that simple, though—sometimes, a body reaches its limit. Each day, you find that part of your brain is dedicated to the pain your body is constantly experiencing. It's hard to accept that God is your healer when you find yourself so broken physically. It also doesn't make sense when someone tells you God knows what He is doing—it certainly doesn't feel like it!

God didn't assign this burden to you because He thought you could handle it. He hurts for you, and the pain you feel stems from the fallen world in which you live. God sent the Holy Spirit to illuminate the darkness. So even if you don't see a bright side, you can rejoice because the Holy Spirit is your light   and He's always available.

. . . .

*Lord, I don't think I can endure this anymore. Thank You for
Your Holy Spirit, who will show up for me just in time.*

Smile Anyway

You have turned my mourning into joyful dancing. You have taken away my clothes of mourning and clothed me with joy.

PSALM 30:11 NLT

. . . .

Have you ever seen someone so happy that it just makes you sick? This person sits there smiling away while the whole world falls apart. You feel obligated to bring this dreamer back to reality. *With all the turmoil going on, how can you possibly be happy?*

Anytime you switch on the television or get a phone call, your muscles tense up, anticipating tragedy. It seems just when you've finished crying about one thing, another calamity presents itself. You can get so used to trauma that moments of brevity feel weird.

When you are deeply entrenched in the despair of this world, happiness isn't a natural response. Only God is able to take your sadness and turn it into joy—which is far better than any fleeting happiness you may stumble upon. When your peace and joy come from God and not the world, then you too will be able to smile anyway.

. . . .

Lord, it's hard for me not to get swept up in the despair I see all around me. I give my sadness to You so that I can radiate Your joy.

Addicting Joy

My dear brothers and sisters, take note of this:
Everyone should be quick to listen, slow to speak and
slow to become angry, because human anger does
not produce the righteousness that God desires.
JAMES 1:19–20 NIV

No one watches the news and breathes a sigh of relief whenever a perpetrator walks away unscathed. When there is a wrong, people want to see that wrong made right. If evil were allowed to go unchecked, chaos would ensue.

Every day, you see people who seem to have no regard for others. Sometimes, their audacity can make your blood boil. You become so angry at what you've seen and heard that you start lashing out in ways you later regret. Even worse, your outburst didn't help. That person didn't change. And that fact leads you right back to anger.

Anger is an addictive emotion. You can get used to feeling it. Instead of lashing out, which can lead to sadness, God says to be slow to react. It is in this moment of hesitation that the Holy Spirit can move. The only way God can show up is if you give Him the chance. Joy follows the justice that God brings. . .and joy is a better addiction than anger.

God, I feel that the anger inside me is justified. I want to enact
my own justice, but I will choose to invite You into the situation
instead. I look forward to my anger turning into joy.

Go to Sleep

*In peace I will lie down and sleep, for you
alone, O LORD, will keep me safe.*
PSALM 4:8 NLT

When you are little, you are taught to say your prayers before bed. As you pulled your teddy bear close, you would say a quick thank-you to God for your day. After a few minutes, you would decide you needed another drink of water, but your father would tell you to go back to sleep. As you laid your head back on your pillow, you would quickly nod off.

Now that you're older, all that has changed. Sleeping is more complicated, and a lot of prayers may get omitted. Responsibilities and worries keep you from relaxing and falling asleep. When your eyes close, you are met with the images of all your unfinished duties. Threatening nightmares swirl in your mind until the alarm goes off the next morning.

Dwelling on daily life won't help you doze off. The rest you need can only come from the peace of Jesus. You don't have to sleep with one eye open or be concerned about tomorrow. Instead, you can rejoice because you are God's child. When your Father tells you to sleep, you know it's time to go to bed.

*Father God, it is hard to get good sleep when I am burdened. I choose
to give it all to You, trusting Your direction so that I can rest.*

You're Correct

"For I know the plans I have for you," says the
LORD. "They are plans for good and not for
disaster, to give you a future and a hope."
JEREMIAH 29:11 NLT

. . . .

Some loss is unavoidable. But then there's that type of loss that begs the question "What if?" You are constantly left wondering if where you are now is where you should be. If that decision you made was actually the best one. Some memories leave a huge smile on your face, but others seem like tormenting reminders of what could have been.

When you are having a difficulty, the natural reaction is to think of a scenario in which you'd no longer face it. Your situation seems to confirm the wrongness of your choice. Obviously, if you had chosen another path, you wouldn't be on this one.

But God loves you however (and wherever) you are—in any stage of life and in any circumstance. This does not imply that there isn't work to be done. It simply means that regardless of where you are now, you can rejoice because your path is filled with hope. You don't have to question your past decisions—as long as you're choosing God in the present, you're correct.

. . . .

Father God, I often wonder where I would be had I made different
choices. Instead, I will rejoice because You are my best decision.

Guarding Gratitude

And give thanks for everything to God the Father
in the name of our Lord Jesus Christ.
EPHESIANS 5:20 NLT

• •

The Louvre, a museum in Paris, France, is heavily guarded to prevent anyone from tampering with the priceless artifacts inside. Countless security systems and skilled, watchful guards are peppered all throughout the building. If something happens, the guards are the first to jump in and protect these cultural treasures.

Obviously, it makes sense to guard those types of objects. But what about when it comes to your thoughts? Thoughts lead to emotions, which then lead to actions. And out of all the thoughts you have in a day, the negative ones tend to have greater sticking power. Consequently, your positive thoughts must be protected.

Gratitude is the guardian of your joy. Safeguarding your joy goes deeper than being grateful for what didn't happen—it means being grateful that God has the opportunity to get all the glory. It means being thankful because you know that the same God who showed up for you before will show up for you again. When bad things happen, let gratitude jump in first.

• •

Father God, it's easy for me to focus on all the negative
things that are going on. Instead, I thank You and
praise Your name for all that is right!

Waiting On Eternity

*"And this is the way to have eternal life—
to know you, the only true God, and Jesus
Christ, the one you sent to earth."*

John 17:3 nlt

• •

Waiting. In general, people don't like it. People don't get up and think about how happy they are to get behind twenty other people in the coffee shop—they think about how great that first sip of coffee will taste. And for coffee lovers, the wait is worth it.

But waiting isn't just for coffee lines. You may find yourself waiting for a better job, a marriage, or even retirement. Regardless of what you're waiting for, it's frustrating. It feels like you are at a standstill, and all you want is for it to be your turn.

Well, it *is* your turn, and there's no line for God's kingdom. All you have to do is believe and serve. There's no status you have to achieve for eternal life—you already have it in Jesus Christ! Don't feel hopeless waiting for your start; rejoice that your start happened on a cross over two thousand years ago.

• •

*Lord, it's tempting to believe that I don't have everything
I need, but I know You gave me what I needed most.
For that, I will praise and thank You for all eternity.*

A Strong Weakness

That is why, for Christ's sake, I delight in weaknesses,
in insults, in hardships, in persecutions, in difficulties.
For when I am weak, then I am strong.

2 CORINTHIANS 12:10 NIV

There is a contest being held somewhere right now. Its goal? To determine who is the strongest. To see who can throw a tire the farthest. To see who can lift that car off the ground. When all is said and done, the mightiest contestant will emerge victorious.

While you may not be able to lift a car, you still want to be seen as strong—if not physically, then definitely emotionally. Nobody wants to be seen as weak. People only admire those who can't be pushed around.

To an onlooker, it would've seemed like Jesus was being made to do things He didn't want to. Even when He was on the cross, the thief questioned why Jesus didn't use His authority. Jesus knew that in His weakness, God would get the glory. When the Holy Spirit is guiding you, you don't need to worry about appearing weak. You can rejoice, boasting in the glory of God.

Lord, I can feel so weak at times, considering what I'm up against.
But I know I'm not alone—it's only because of You that I'm strong.

Seeing Green

Peter saw him and said to Jesus, "But Lord, what about this one?" Jesus said, "If I want this one to wait until I come, what is that to you? You follow Me."

JOHN 21:21–22 NLV

Before Christ ascended, He walked with the disciples and ministered to them. In His conversation with Peter, He explained how Peter's ministry would continue and bring glory to God. However, Peter was more interested in what would happen to another disciple. In response to this jealousy, Jesus simply said, "What is that to you? You follow Me."

Covetousness, envy, and resentfulness are all a part of the dreaded green-eyed monster. The more connected you are on social media or the more "boastful Bettys" you know, the harder you'll have to fight to obtain contentment.

It is time to stop looking to your left and right and instead remember who you follow. There's no need to worry about whether you're ahead of others. The one you follow, Jesus Christ, is infinitely more important than anyone's status. There's no need to be jealous when you serve a good Father—only joyous. And instead of seeing a green-eyed monster, you may just see more people to serve.

Father God, I sometimes compare myself to others. I praise You for Your love that releases me from that bondage.

How Much?

*But the Holy Spirit produces this kind
of fruit in our lives: love, joy, peace,
patience, kindness, goodness, faithfulness,
gentleness, and self-control. There is
no law against these things!*
GALATIANS 5:22–23 NLT

There is a type of strawberry called the Bijin-Hime. Priced at four thousand dollars, it is one of the most expensive fruits in the world. There are roughly five hundred made per season, and they are three times larger than a regular strawberry. Eating one of them would definitely lighten your wallet.

The fruits of the Holy Spirit are much more valuable. . .but they can also seem just as unattainable. The thought of trying to display any of these characteristics during a stressful moment can feel like a tall order. In fact, many of us feel the exact opposite of these fruits on most days.

The fruits of the Spirit are more than feelings—they are the by-products of God's love. Even if you spent all day attempting to display them, it wouldn't be enough. If you contend for joy, you may not find it, but when you surrender to the available love of God, joy will find you.

And *that* won't hurt your wallet.

*Father God, I know I need You in order to follow
Your example. Even though I fall short sometimes,
I know Your love puts me back where I need to be.*

No Filter

She is clothed with strength and dignity;
she can laugh at the days to come.
PROVERBS 31:25 NIV

It's hard to measure up to someone who's perfect. Now that editing, lighting, and filters are so accessible, every woman has the ability to radiate perfection. . .online, at least. Deep down, you know it's not completely real, but you still feel as if you'll never measure up.

The book of Proverbs tells what a virtuous woman consists of. One of her many qualities is being able to laugh at whatever comes her way. This means that regardless of what news she hears, the bills that come, or any health problems that arise, she maintains the ability to laugh. With all of her attributes, she seems flawless.

But the virtuous woman isn't perfect—she simply knows whom to put her faith in. God wants the same stability and joy for you. The security you crave can be found only in Him. It's not about forcing a smile or grinning and bearing it. It's about knowing you are free in Christ and being able to laugh at anything that tries to bind you. Being a Proverbs 31 woman is not unattainable. It happens naturally when you look at Jesus—no filter.

Father God, it is tempting to make my life appear
perfect. Please help me keep my eyes on You and not
on the empty excellence I see on my phone.

It's a Process

Yet you, LORD, are our Father. We are the clay,
you are the potter; we are all the work of your hand.

ISAIAH 64:8 NIV

So far, the story of your life has been rough. You definitely relate to the term "wrong side of the tracks." The happy times were few and far between, and the dark times play more clearly in your mind than any of the bright spots. While you are grateful when you have stability, it's always accompanied with the fear of losing it. You find yourself wishing that something could give you safety and love.

Then you hear about Jesus. Even though you believe He loved you enough to die for you, it's still hard to accept. Every time you look in the mirror, you're reminded of all the hurt that's inside you. You have no idea why God loves you. You feel dejected.

The reason He loves you and sent His Son to die for you is simple: you are the work of His hands. When you let God work through you, there is no reason to be concerned about how flawed you are—just joyous at what's to come. Seeing a finished piece of clay—molded and glossed to perfection—is beautiful. Just don't forget the work it took to get there.

Lord, while I don't feel worthy of You sometimes,
I know that isn't true. I will trust that You love
me and that my past will be for Your glory.

What You're Made For

You have given me greater joy than those who have
abundant harvests of grain and new wine.

PSALM 4:7 NLT

• •

You ever sit and wonder why you can't just be happy? Everyone does at one point or another. Being sad gets old, and you long to be cheerful. It feels like you're bringing down everyone else around you, and you don't want to be a drag.

What's frustrating is that you haven't even been complacent about your mood. You've tried many things to lift your spirits—from therapy to a multitude of new hobbies—but nothing seems to work. Each time you attempt something that might inspire a smile, it's never as good as what you imagined. These endeavors only lead to more emptiness.

You long for happiness but are made for joy. The reason that nothing on this earth seems to fulfill you is because it simply can't. Following God is better than the promotion, new car, or latest gadget. The joy that comes from communion with Him is better than any worldly thing. So when you're tempted to envy someone else's temporary happiness, just remember what you were made for.

• •

God, I don't want any counterfeit goods this world
can give me. The things You have for me are far better,
and I receive them with true joy in my heart.

Hopeful Truth

And hope does not put us to shame, because God's love has been poured out into our hearts through the Holy Spirit, who has been given to us.
ROMANS 5:5 NIV

The word *hope* is everywhere. It can be found along with the words *faith* and *love*, written in a beautiful font on a piece of wood, in many homes throughout America. It is a reminder through difficult times that things will get better.

Things might not be getting better, though. Your problems aren't fading, and any relief is fleeting. You've created a beautiful narrative in your head of what things will look like once this circumstance has passed. The problem is that this manufactured hope can cloud the truth.

The hope that God gives, however, matches truth. That's why it will never leave you distraught or ashamed. When the Holy Spirit guides you, you know you are loved, so the truth doesn't cause fear. Hope isn't some spiritual bypass that instantly makes everything okay. The hope God offers gives you joy because it's the truth. . .and the truth sets you free.

Lord Jesus, I don't want to rely on my own invented hope. I praise You and thank You for the true hope You give—the only hope that will bring me freedom.

Joyful Aroma

I will praise you as long as I live, and in your name I will
lift up my hands. I will be fully satisfied as with the richest
of foods; with singing lips my mouth will praise you.
PSALM 63:4–5 NIV

The drive home seemed to take longer than normal, and you are eager to get your evening started. It's been a long day, and you want to relax and take it easy. As soon as you open the door, the most delicious aroma fills your nose. Dinner is ready—what a wonderful surprise!

If that's ever happened to you, you'll probably never forget it. Although it was a surprise, that lovely person's deed became obvious as soon as you opened the door. Even though you couldn't see the food at first, the smell gave it away.

Joy is no different. When you are truly joyous, there's no hiding it. After food has been prepared, you can smell it. When you embrace the truth of God's promises, your joy will be evident. You won't be able to contain your praises to Him, because He is good. And just like every food has its own aroma, every facet of God's truth brings its own joyful aroma with sweet praise.

Lord, thank You for helping me nourish my joy with strong, healthy
truth. All my praise is for You and to bring glory to Your kingdom.

Satiate

Your words were found, and I ate them, and your
words became to me a joy and the delight of my heart,
for I am called by your name, O LORD, God of hosts.
JEREMIAH 15:16 ESV

· ·

Margaery's fingers drummed on her steering wheel. It seemed like she'd been waiting on her food for twenty minutes—it had only been two. Her lunch breaks weren't that long, and she was incredibly hungry. As she pulled up to the drive-thru window, she quickly paid for her food and started eating before she even drove off. The server never even heard a thank-you.

Getting so hungry that you become angry—or *hangry*, as it has come to be known—is very common. Rage starts welling up within because your need isn't being met. You are so short with others that you end up apologizing later. You're just not yourself when you're hungry.

Your spirit gets hungry too, but the food it craves is the Word of God. Just as it wouldn't be wise to send malnourished troops into battle, you can't expect people to just grit their teeth and choose joy. Joy is the outcome of a relationship with God.

So if you're hangry, eat food; but if you're empty, let God's Word satiate you.

· ·

Lord, I want a deeper relationship with You. Please help me
make that a priority so that my spirit is filled with You.

Red, Clear, and Blue

And the Lord's servant must not be quarrelsome but kind to everyone, able to teach, patiently enduring evil, correcting his opponents with gentleness.

2 TIMOTHY 2:24–25 ESV

World history has a lot of baggage. With every war, soldiers had to choose a side—and time would tell if they chose correctly. It's easy to look back and see who was on the right side of history, but what about the battles we're embroiled in today?

There's always some polarizing topic that will instantly gain you enemies and friends, no matter which side you choose. People no longer bond over a list of favorites but rather what news channel they tune in to. One bumper sticker shouts the name of one candidate; the next promotes another. And both owners think they alone have all the facts.

When you are a child of God, both your history and your future are different. The kingdom you belong to has a perfect leader, so there's no cause for dissension. You don't have to choose a side that the world gives—that will only steal your joy. There's no need to get riled up, because the solution is already available: it's God's love. And God's love can't be any clearer.

God, I'm sorry for letting the politics of this world steal my joy. You alone are my Lord, and I thank You for helping me love like You do.

The Bumblebee Flies Anyway

And so my heart is glad. My soul is full of joy.
My body also will rest without fear.
PSALM 16:9 NLV

- -

At first glance, it doesn't appear that the bumblebee's tiny wings and chubby body would be conducive to flight. Still, there goes the bumblebee from flower to flower, doing what pollinators do best. The fact that it doesn't appear like they should be able to fly doesn't faze them—they do it anyway.

While science can explain how bumblebees fly, it's still fascinating because nobody explained this to the bee! Humans are slightly more complex. Wouldn't it be nice if someone occasionally explained to you how to keep going? Because of everything you see and hear, joy seems elusive. You feel heavy and desperate. The weight of the world doesn't feel good on your shoulders.

Give yourself permission to rest in Jesus. When everything is going wrong, it's okay to be glad in Him. Even when your situation seems to demand misery, all things are possible with God. If the bumblebee can fly anyway, you can let go of fear and rejoice.

- -

God, joy is the last thing I feel right now. However, I give my
fear directly to You, eager to rejoice in You and in who You are.

Drop Anchor

"You didn't choose me. I chose you. I appointed you to go and produce lasting fruit, so that the Father will give you whatever you ask for, using my name."
JOHN 15:16 NLT

. . . .

Imagine if boats didn't have anchors. There'd be nothing to secure the boat's position, leaving the boat free to drift far away from its destination. The reason an anchor is dropped on a boat is because without it, the boat would not be safe.

Similarly, insecurity can destroy relationships. Before you know it, both sides are slinging accusations, and an already rough situation continues to devolve. In those moments, it's hard to recall your goals or purpose. You crave reassurance but keep running into complacency. You want guidance, but the waters ahead are shrouded in mystery.

But God, the Creator of the universe, chose you—and He did it with intention. He has a purpose and calling for your life. His plan for you will help glorify and further His kingdom. Your anchor is in the love, joy, and peace God offers you through Jesus Christ. When you're feeling uncertain, check where you last dropped your anchor.

. . . .

Lord Jesus, all my emotions can make me forget where my stability comes from. Even if it feels like I am drifting, I believe You are my anchor.

Accepted

But by the grace of God I am what I am, and his grace to
me was not without effect. No, I worked harder than all of
them—yet not I, but the grace of God that was with me.
1 Corinthians 15:10 NIV

. . . .

Getting called last during gym is not fun—it makes you feel like you aren't good enough. Not only do you have to play the game, you also have to deal with the shame of feeling unwanted. Such scenarios don't lead to confidence.

Getting called first during gym, however, is the perfect scenario. Everyone around you can see that you are wanted. They don't just want to play with you—they *need* you on their team to succeed. No one has trouble seeing your confidence.

Not everyone will want you on their team, especially if you're following God. When others reject you for trying to show God's love to them, it's not you they're rejecting—it's God. On the other hand, if everyone wants to be around you because you make them feel loved, it's not you they admire—it's Jesus. Both self-inflation and self-degradation can get in the way of joy. When your confidence rests in your Creator, teams don't matter—you know you are fully accepted.

. . . .

Father God, I believe You fully accept me because of Your Son. I give
my pride to You and ask to be more aware of Your love instead.

Serving Joy

"You call me 'Teacher' and 'Lord,' and rightly so, for that is what I am. Now that I, your Lord and Teacher, have washed your feet, you also should wash one another's feet."

JOHN 13:13–14 NIV

• •

It is disheartening when loved ones don't meet your needs. You've made it very clear—maybe even a little *too* clear—what is needed to rectify the situation. But they simply don't seem to care. It's extremely hard not to get offended.

When people overlook you, the last thing you think about is how to serve them. Doing anything for them just doesn't make sense. If you're not their priority, why should they be your principal concern? Relationships should be equal.

But relationships will never be equal on this side of heaven. One party will often feel superior to the other. When Jesus washed His disciples' feet, He wasn't thinking about who would wash His feet. Even though Jesus and His disciples had the same need, He tended to them first. He was a servant to those He loved.

Not feeling cherished can steal your joy, but meeting the other person's needs can bring it back.

• •

Father God, it's nigh impossible to place others' needs before my own. Please help me be a better example of Your love so that I may serve others well.

Fruit

"Yes, I am the vine; you are the branches. Those who remain in me, and I in them, will produce much fruit. For apart from me you can do nothing."
JOHN 15:5 NLT

• •

It appears as if everyone around you has a YouTube channel, thousands of Facebook friends, and hundreds of stunning pictures on Instagram. You'd love to belong to such an important world—a world where you'd feel valued. However, making videos is out of your element, you don't know that many people, and most of your phone's pictures are fuzzy.

Pursuing a life of influence is extremely appealing. Having followers makes you feel significant and important. People looking to you for advice makes you feel like you've "leveled up" in life. It's hard to mind the fact that others are looking to you as an example.

As appealing as a life of influence is, a life of fruitfulness is more rewarding. Abiding in God will give you the purpose and joy you crave. God will dwell in you. . .and there's nothing insignificant about that! Serving God may not come with all the fame, but it's fruit that feeds people, not followers.

• •

Lord God, thank You for working through me to help further Your kingdom. I want all the glory to be Yours because that will bring joy not only to me but others as well.

Little Foxes

"Catch the foxes for us, the little foxes that spoil the vineyards, for our vineyards are in blossom."
SONG OF SOLOMON 2:15 ESV

Imagination allows you to create and construct beyond what you see. From airplanes to the pyramids, dreaming helped make it a reality. Someone had a thought and convinced others to join in, and with time, their idea was realized.

Building a pyramid or taking credit for the Boeing 747 would be great. But that's not how your imagination often works, though. Your thoughts and ideas sometimes leave you feeling sad. It would be lovely to dream positively, but more often than not, you find yourself dwelling on all that could go wrong.

In the Song of Solomon, foxes are used to illustrate the havoc that can be wreaked whenever you dwell on the wrong things. These musings must be stopped in their tracks. If they are allowed to run amok, they can turn your joy into devastation. God wants your mind to rest safely in Him. If you tend to be anxious and worry, remind those thoughts of whom you serve.

While you may not know what the fox says, you can certainly catch them.

Lord, my thoughts and imagination can run rampant.
I will praise You and walk with You where these
fearful little daydreams mean nothing.

Fetch the Water

"The LORD GOD is my strength and my song, and he has become my salvation." With joy you will draw water from the wells of salvation.

ISAIAH 12:2–3 ESV

. . . .

Getting water from a well requires stamina. Raising the full bucket, transferring the water to a container, and then hauling the container is no small task. While it is laborious, it is essential. Your body can't survive without being hydrated.

Today, have you noticed any signs of thirst? It's most likely not for actual water—that's an easy fix. No, you may be experiencing dryness in other areas, such as work, home, or relationships. Quenching that thirst is more complex. Many have tried—and failed—to quell the parched landscape of their life. This landscape is constantly changing, and it is hard to keep up.

Even though areas of your life might be so dry that a fire could break out, the water God provides will extinguish them. Maintaining joy requires stamina and hard work, but God's wells never run empty. If you feel parched from the flames, all you need to do is fetch the water.

. . . .

Lord Jesus, thank You for the stamina that comes from Your love. I praise You for being my constant source of love and support as I face the fallen world I live in.

Hot and Cold

*"I know your works: you are neither cold nor hot. Would that
you were either cold or hot! So, because you are lukewarm,
and neither hot nor cold, I will spit you out of my mouth."*
REVELATION 3:15–16 ESV

Laodicea, a Roman province of Asia, had everything it needed to
thrive. It had a vast population and a booming textile industry, both
of which needed water to flourish. Laodicea, along with Colossae and
Hierapolis, all had very distinct water sources.

Colossae lay near the foot of the mountain, so it had access to
the cold, fresh water that flowed down from the top. Hierapolis sat
next to spectacular hot springs that provided mineral-rich waters. But
Laodicea's water was lukewarm and gritty after traveling miles in an
aqueduct. While their water greatly benefited their textile industry,
drinking it would cause you to vomit.

When John wrote today's verses to Laodicea, he was talking about
usefulness. Even though the city had everything it needed, Colossae's
and Hierapolis' water supplies were superior because they benefited
others. No one sought out the water from Laodicea.

Living for yourself is about as useful as lukewarm water. When you
are selfish, your joy can be lost. Nourishing and replenishing others is
part of your calling in Jesus Christ. So be cold for Jesus and revitalize
the lost, but also be hot, comforting others with His love. Be both!

*God, I want to be useful to You. I ask for Your Holy Spirit to
work through me so that I can help everyone who needs You.*

The World's Greatest

*"The greatest among you shall be your servant.
Whoever exalts himself will be humbled, and
whoever humbles himself will be exalted."*

MATTHEW 23:11–12 ESV

Little Mckenzie wasn't feeling well, so her grandmother came to get her from school. When they arrived at her grandma's house, the couch was ready with pillows and blankets. Mckenzie ate homemade nuggets and buttered corn for lunch while she sipped on sweet tea. As the cartoons played on the television, she felt better. And when she grew up, she never forgot it.

When you think of the people who have affected you the most, chances are, they are the ones who served you. They went out of their way to make you more comfortable. They didn't assume their own business was more important than you. Because they put aside pride and humbled themselves, you remember them.

Going out of your way for others is not always easy, but the resulting joy is immense. People won't forget a first-hand encounter with the love of Jesus. You are the vessel for that. When you serve others, joy is not the only benefit—that "World's Greatest. . ." coffee mug may just start meaning something to the person you've helped.

Father God, You gave the perfect example of servitude. Help me push past my comfort zone and into what is loving and helpful for others.

Spared No Expense

Since he did not spare even his own Son but gave him up for us all, won't he also give us everything else?
ROMANS 8:32 NLT

• •

If you are a guest at a dinner party, this means you're not the one who will see the bill. The evening is meant for you to enjoy yourself—the price tag just isn't your concern. Each entrée and dessert is all yours to enjoy. The bill belongs to the host.

It'd be absurd to invite people to a party and then charge them for each little item. The guests would most likely not stay very long. While they might want to spend time with the one who invited them, they would worry about the overall cost.

When you become a child of God, He withholds nothing from you. There's no need to be concerned about what you owe—it was paid for on the cross. Love, joy, peace, patience, and many other wonderful gifts are yours. God made certain that you could enjoy a full relationship with Him, and to do that, He spared no expense.

• •

God, I know I have access to the life You want for me because of Your Son, Jesus Christ. I ask daily for Your grace that makes this possible.

Upgrade

*"The kingdom of heaven is like treasure hidden in a field.
When a man found it, he hid it again, and then in his
joy went and sold all he had and bought that field."*

MATTHEW 13:44 NIV

. . . .

Rebecca heard a knock at the door and went to answer it. The visitor politely asked her to give away her home and belongings. She smiled and quickly obliged, no questions asked.

What's wrong with the above scenario? For starters, a real-life Rebecca would ask *tons* of questions and probably call the authorities. Freely giving up everything you've worked for doesn't make any sense. The benefit would have to be substantial indeed.

However, if the visitor offered you many times over the worth of what you own, would you hesitate? Probably not. You'd feel no need to look back as you prepared for your new, upgraded life.

The kingdom of heaven is the greatest treasure there is. Whatever you feel you have to give up to serve God, you can do so joyfully because it will be worth it. Your perfect prize is found in serving God. When you let go of your old life, God will replace it with the ultimate upgrade.

. . . .

*Lord, I am losing joy over the things I think matter. I ask that Your
Holy Spirit guide me because I know You are my true wealth.*

Sweet Relief

*You give them relief from troubled times
until a pit is dug to capture the wicked.*
PSALM 94:13 NLT

· ·

Odds are, you focused on the latter half of this verse. The fact that the wicked will end up in a pit eases your soul. Right now, you may be imagining your least favorite individual(s) walking along. . .and then suddenly free-falling into a gaping hole. They would then be the pit's problem, not yours. You'd be able to continue your day without sparing them a thought.

The first half of this scripture, though, is far more interesting. It has the audacity to suggest that during troubled times, God will give relief. This can be hard to believe while you're dealing with the same annoying situations and people. People can't be changed, and some circumstances can't be avoided. How can relief come when circumstances won't budge?

God is your consolation, and the respite you need is found in Him. The people around you don't have to change, and your joy doesn't have to get stolen. There's no need to waste your time wondering when other people will get their just desserts—you can partake in the sweetness of the Lord anytime you want.

· ·

*Lord, help me focus less on others' fallen nature.
I recognize that I fall short too, and I praise You for Your
grace and mercy that's available in those moments.*

Voice Mail

"Then you will call on me and come and
pray to me, and I will listen to you."

JEREMIAH 29:12 NIV

. . . .

Businesses employ numerous strategies to get the public's attention. From using a wacky inflatable arm guy to painting their signs with bright colors, companies try their best to pique your interest and draw you in. Ignoring these institutions' efforts is harmless—they do not affect your day, much less your life.

Business, however, is not relationships. When loved ones ignore your bid for attention, it absolutely affects your life. Resentment starts to well up. The negative voices in your head start sinking in. Every second you spend waiting for a response makes your heart ache a bit more.

When you call upon the name of Jesus, He hears you. Every time you take a moment to connect with God, you don't have to wonder where He is or what He is doing. God is right there, listening to every word you say. . .even the bad ones. In the presence of the Lord, there is joy because He is aware.

So when the connection you need to make goes to voice mail, call on Him—He'll answer.

. . . .

Father God, I have many needs and desires that are
pressing, but Your timing is perfect. I will have peace and
joy while waiting because I know You have heard me.

Sharing Joy

Be happy with those who are happy,
and weep with those who weep.
ROMANS 12:15 NLT

. . . .

Hearing happy news can sometimes be difficult. While you are excited for your friend, you can't help but wish it were you. It would be really nice to catch a break like that. You start thinking it *should* be you. As you hear yourself congratulating that person, it sounds hollow. The resentfulness wells up inside, and it's difficult to shove it back down.

Conversely, being with a friend during a crisis can be just as hard. It's not that you don't want to help—you simply don't know how. Offering your presence is essential, but if you're not careful, the weight of your friend's problem can drag you down too.

Empathy is precious because it allows you to relate to others and their situations. God wants you to have a soft heart, but this doesn't mean you have to hand over your joy. The Holy Spirit is accessible at any given moment to humble pride and ease sorrow. Instead of letting these situations take your joy, you can share it instead.

. . . .

God, thank You for helping me look past the way I feel,
regardless of the news I hear. I want to be an example of Your
joy in any circumstance so that others can feel Your love.

Office or Throne?

All honor and glory to God forever and ever!
He is the eternal King, the unseen one who
never dies; he alone is God. Amen.
1 TIMOTHY 1:17 NLT

. . . .

Instead of waiting on God's promises, the Israelites insisted that they have a leader just like other nations. That type of government would evolve into the dream of democracy that many still seek today. This democracy is composed of different parties with different beliefs. And every four years, a vote is held to choose a new commander and chief to guide the nation—an overwhelming responsibility, to be sure.

To help you choose, a constant flow of information and data is thrown at you at every turn. If you've already decided, any other opinions can anger you. Disagreements can get so heated that friendships are destroyed and families are fractured. Coexisting doesn't seem possible when everyone's beliefs are so fundamentally different.

But there's good news: you don't have to be a part of this vicious cycle. Rather than being angry toward others who oppose what you feel is right, you can have joy in letting the Holy Spirit guide you toward His righteousness. God is your eternal King, not a temporary one. And He leads from a throne, not an office.

. . . .

God, it's hard not to get sucked into the world's current affairs.
Still, I choose to serve You and be an example of joy in the turmoil.

Unmovable Joy

When God says, "Once more," He means He will take
away everything of this world that can be shaken
so the things that cannot be shaken will be left.
HEBREWS 12:27 NLV

When rock climbers are scaling a mountain, safety is priority. They make sure they are secure before they proceed further. That way, if a rock slips underneath them, their harness—which is attached to something that cannot be moved—rescues them.

Life can be as unstable as rock climbing. It can feel like anytime you try to find sure footing, the earth shifts beneath you. In those moments, you try your best to make things return to what you are used to. In your opinion, everything was fine the way it was—there's no need for change.

God is the only one you can rely on not to change. So when the ground shakes, that's a perfect time to look for the new solid ground that God is forming. Don't trust the worry that can come with change; instead, receive joy from the Holy Spirit as He guides you. It may feel like you might be slipping, but Jesus cannot be moved, and you are firmly in Him.

Lord, even when my next move crumbles beneath my hands, I trust
that I am firmly in You. Thank You for Your love and guidance.

Image of Love

"Love each other. Just as I have loved you, you should love each other. Your love for one another will prove to the world that you are my disciples."

JOHN 13:34 NLT

It's true that opposites can attract, but sharing similarities is important as well. When you have common ground with others, it can deepen your bond. There is a certain ease in being around them, and conversation flows well. You don't find yourself trying too hard or struggling to relate to them—it seems as though you are all cut from the same cloth.

Encountering others who have different viewpoints than you just doesn't go as smoothly. When you believe that your stance is the correct one, that makes those who don't agree with you incorrect. And when you associate being incorrect with being unacceptable, your dislike can turn into hate.

God made you in His image, and God loves all people, not just some of them. It is tempting to create a god in your head that likes what you like and hates what you hate. Your joy can't increase when you limit God's love. The calling on a disciple of Christ is love! If you find God agreeing with you a lot, you might want to look into what you can agree with Him about.

Lord, I want to know You better and understand Your likes and dislikes. Help me open my heart to the perfect love You want to work through me.

Rules to Follow

"When you obey my commandments, you remain in my love, just as I obey my Father's commandments and remain in his love. I have told you these things so that you will be filled with my joy. Yes, your joy will overflow!"

JOHN 15:10–11 NLT

When you were younger, it was clear that there were rules to follow. Disobedience meant time-outs or no dessert for dinner. When you stuck to those rules, your parents told you yes. You didn't have to beg and plead for what you wanted. But if you rebelled, you knew better than to ask for anything—the answer would always be no.

Obedience can give you amazing privileges, but when you grow older, submitting to authority becomes harder. You have questions, and you insist upon understanding the "why" behind any command. This is not unreasonable. Humans, after all, are imperfect, and blind obedience can be dangerous.

But when you heed the Holy Spirit and follow God, it's more than obedience—it becomes second nature. It's this nature that identifies you as belonging to God. It is then that He takes immense pleasure in you, His creation. God's approval brings more joy than any rule to be followed, and no one can stop the overflow.

Father God, obeying when I have questions is hard.
But I will trust in You because I belong to You.

111

Speak Life

Anxiety weighs down the heart,
but a kind word cheers it up.
PROVERBS 12:25 NIV

. . . .

If you saw a guy walking down the street muttering to himself, you might be concerned. Depending on the time of day, you might even find yourself walking a bit faster. Part of you wants to know what's wrong, but the other part of you is concerned for your safety.

Though you may not do it audibly, you speak to yourself. . .and it can be just as crazy. The things you say about yourself would probably send a normal person to therapy. Worry and anxiety lie at the root of most of your thoughts, and they weigh heavy on your soul. You'd love to feel lighter, but life is a heavy burden to bear.

At this point, you need affectionate words that nourish you—and it can't come from someone else. The Holy Spirit has to guide you away from the negative self-talk so that your joy can be full. Nowhere does the Bible say you can only focus on what makes you miserable. As wrong as everything may be, God's words of love can make it right.

Now that's something to talk about!

. . . .

Lord, what You say about me is the truth. Regardless of what
my thoughts may tell me, I will let Your Holy Spirit guide me.

No Appointment Needed

You know when I sit and when I rise; you perceive my thoughts from afar. You discern my going out and my lying down; you are familiar with all my ways.

PSALM 139:2–3 NIV

. . . .

Picture someone famous whom you admire, and now imagine you are in that person's circle. This celebrity knows not only your name but your favorite foods and your favorite color. The celebrity listens intently to everything you say, answers the phone whenever you call, and is never too busy for you. You are able to confide in this person.

How likely do you think that is?

Sometimes, it feels like your regular friends and family are famous. No matter how hard you try to connect with them, it doesn't work out. You've known these people since you were young, but they feel like strangers today. You feel like you need to make an appointment just to hang out with them.

God thinks of you constantly. He knows everything about you, including your favorite food and color. It would be impossible for you to even count the number of thoughts God has about you in a day. And even better, every one of those thoughts is good. You can learn all about these good thoughts through prayer—no appointment needed!

. . . .

Father God, I'm so grateful that Your thoughts about me are good. I will continue to seek You when others leave me wanting.

Where Is God?

Jesus replied, "All who love me will do what I say. My Father will love them, and we will come and make our home with each of them."

JOHN 14:23 NLT

• •

Synagogues, churches, and Christian temples are all places built for worship. Each building contains painstaking levels of detail, including the use of stained glass. All are intended to help you draw closer to God and approach Him with penitence.

Being able to fellowship with other believers ministers to your spirit, and it's an opportunity to lift each other up as well. But as good as this might sound, it's not always probable. Attending service might be hard—either because you're busy, or because you've been wounded in the past by other churchgoers. Regardless of the reason, the formalities of a place of worship might be hard to stomach.

God wants to dwell in you, not just in a building. There's no special building you must enter in order to experience His presence. When you are His child, He goes with you wherever you go. You can delight in the fact that God is in your heart. It might not look like a temple, but you can praise Him there anyway.

• •

Lord, please help me remember that there are no formalities with You, because You dwell in me. Help me make my heart a comfortable place for You to live.

Better Than Superglue

And I am convinced that nothing can ever separate
us from God's love. Neither death nor life, neither
angels nor demons, neither our fears for today
nor our worries about tomorrow—not even the
powers of hell can separate us from God's love.
ROMANS 8:38 NLT

Superglue can fix just about anything that's broken. It can tolerate extreme conditions, absorb shock, bond to countless materials, and stick until the end of time. If you use superglue, chances are that your fingers have stuck together. If so, you know it is no easy fix.

Wouldn't it be nice if you could use superglue to fix your daily life? When a relationship breaks, all you'd have to do is pull out that silver tube and put it back together. Or when a heart gets shattered—whether through neglect or intentional hurt—a little bit of glue would ensure it never breaks again.

God's love works better than superglue. Regardless of how many pieces you find yourself in, He can put you back together. Brokenness is burdensome, but when God's love restores you, nothing can separate you from it again.

Lord, I've been trying to fix the pieces of my life by
myself. I ask for Your restorative love to mend me
and make me whole so that You get the glory.

Joy Unspeakable

*"But let him who boasts boast in this, that he understands
and knows me, that I am the LORD who practices
steadfast love, justice, and righteousness in the earth.
For in these things I delight, declares the LORD."*

JEREMIAH 9:24 ESV

It's adorable to see children boasting about their accomplishments—such as handprint artwork or a new song. It's a different story when adults brag on themselves. Within the first few minutes of talking to them, you've heard enough. There is no humbleness in them.

There are some situations, though, that you can't help but put on airs. You want absolutely everyone to know something good is happening for you. It's not that you don't want to be modest—it's that you don't know how not to share your success.

If you know God, you'll find it hard to keep quiet about Him. When you passionately love Him and spend time with Him, your knowledge of who He is grows deeper. The joy you have in God will be so full that it never goes away—you'll feel you *must* share His glory with everyone.

Just don't be surprised if words aren't good enough to convey all that He is.

*God, I praise You for who You are and all that You
do. I want my knowledge of You to grow deeper
so that I can share that joy with others.*

More Than Words

Likewise the Spirit helps us in our weakness. For we do not know what to pray for as we ought, but the Spirit himself intercedes for us with groanings too deep for words.
ROMANS 8:26 ESV

A poor deer stops completely in its tracks, blinded by the headlights of your car. The look on its face is completely expressionless. Perhaps it feels bad about the fact that it could potentially be in your way. Or maybe, like you, it's trying to get home for dinner. Either way, your vehicle caught it unaware, and you ended up in a staring contest.

When faced with certain situations, you may not even know where to start. Help would be beneficial, obviously, but you're unsure of what you even need assistance with. All you can offer is a blank stare. You start relating to that deer.

When you need help, that is the perfect time to pray. The Holy Spirit is there to tell God all the things you don't know how to say. Your big feelings are perfectly expressed to God through His Spirit. You can have great joy in knowing there will never be a break in communication with God.

If you don't have the words, the Holy Spirit definitely does.

Lord, my feelings are too big for words. I thank You that Your Holy Spirit knows how to convey my heart.

Give It Away

You will be enriched in every way so that you can be generous on every occasion, and through us your generosity will result in thanksgiving to God.

2 CORINTHIANS 9:11 NIV

. . . .

If you had a million dollars, the possibilities would be endless. Not only would you be rich, you'd have the power to actualize many of your dreams. But even though that money would solve a lot, it would also raise problems. Many lottery winners have found themselves in serious trouble because of their wealth.

If the Bible gives so many warnings about the love of money, why would a Christian ever want to prosper? With all the pitfalls that wealth can bring, you might start craving a secluded existence. The thought of being able to pay all your bills and still have a fortune left over is nice. . .but at what cost?

The price of prosperity is generosity. God enriches your life so that you are able to directly bless others. Believing in God is synonymous with giving. In order for your joy to be complete, you have to give to others and share in their delight. You have to give it away.

. . . .

Lord, it is because of You that I can be a vessel of joy. Please help me recognize all the ways I can help others.

*Joy Included

"If they hear and serve Him, the rest of their days will be filled with what they need and their years with peace."

JOB 36:11 NLV

. . . .

Soldiers in the army don't have to concern themselves with basic needs. Their food, shelter, and clothing are all provided for them. Consequently, they are able to focus on their job. While this is extremely hard work, the benefits are worth it. They know that if they do what is required, they will reap the rewards.

Enlisting in the army is not always an option, though. And though you work hard, the compensation you receive might leave you wanting more. If your struggle for security were going somewhere, you wouldn't mind the fight. But when you take a step back and look at everything, you feel defeated, like it was all for nothing.

When you follow Jesus, your needs will be met—not only materially but emotionally. The outcome may not look as you think it should (just like the manna didn't to the Israelites), but it satisfies just the same. God takes care of His children, so when you need help, it's already on the way. Obeying God's calling ensures that you'll have everything you need—joy included.

. . . .

Father God, I understand that when I serve You, I will be provided for. While I may not get all I want, I trust You to give me all I need.

Listen While You Work

*"If it is good or bad, we will listen to the voice of the Lord
our God to Whom we are sending you. It will go well
with us if we listen to the voice of the Lord our God."*

JEREMIAH 42:6 NLV

. . . .

It is an uncomfortable feeling to have a conversation with someone
and then not remember a thing about it. It can get even more awkward
when you are asked to recall the exchange. The last thing you want to
be is rude or inconsiderate, but there's simply no way to deny that you
weren't paying attention.

Given the amount of thoughts running through your mind, con-
centrating can be difficult. Try as you might to hear what others are
saying, the things that are most important to you will inevitably drown
everything else out. Getting interrupted is usually tolerable, but never
when the offender is your own brain.

As important as it is for you to hear others, it's even more crucial
to listen to the Lord. Praying in the Holy Spirit can help you focus
and keep your thoughts steady. But because God is the Creator of the
universe, listening to Him can be unnerving. However, you can have
joy because it is all meant for your good. Your mind might be working
overtime, but you can still listen through the noise.

. . . .

*Lord, I want to hear and listen to You better. I ask Your
Holy Spirit to help me focus on and delight in You.*

Nightlight

Jesus spoke to the people once more and said, "I am the light of the world. If you follow me, you won't have to walk in darkness, because you will have the light that leads to life."

JOHN 8:12 NLT

Most children hate being sent to bed. They ask for more kisses and multiple drinks of water to delay bedtime. After goodnight is said and the lights are turned off, their little eyes start to play tricks and they become frightened. At this point, a tired parent will invest in a nightlight.

As difficult as getting a child to sleep is, it's even harder to deal with those "monsters" that a nightlight won't expose. Broken relationships, sickness, moral dilemmas—wouldn't it be wonderful if these things could be fixed with the flip of a switch?

When it comes to such matters, you must follow the light that Jesus offers. Following and believing in God means you can have joy that your path will be bright, no matter how dark it gets outside. You just have to let Him turn on the light—which is brighter than any nightlight.

Lord, it is hard to tell where I am going because I can't see my next step. I will look to You and trust in where You tell me to go.

Loving Correction

"Do not regard lightly the discipline of the Lord, nor be weary when reproved by him. For the Lord disciplines the one he loves, and chastises every son whom he receives."
HEBREWS 12:5–6 ESV

No one likes to be wrong, and people will often go to great lengths to prove themselves right. They gather loads of information to support their position and to use in their defense. For some reason, admitting they were wrong or simply misinformed makes some people cringe on a cellular level.

But the hard truth remains: you can't always be right. Try as you might to stand your ground, you just can't change the facts. Most people want to be humble, but no one likes being humbled. It's frustrating to be told you acted incorrectly, and it can also make you resentful of the one who properly informs you.

When God convicts your heart and corrects you, He does so out of pure love. This means you are even closer to Him than a friend: you are His precious daughter. While it's difficult to change and grow, saying you're sorry doesn't equal defeat—it is an opportunity for joy to move in your life.

If God convicts you, don't feel guilty. Feel love.

God, it's hard for me to receive correction because I don't like being wrong. Instead of feeling shame, I will find joy in Your admonition.

EXIT

Let no one say when he is tempted, "I am being tempted by God," for God cannot be tempted with evil, and he himself tempts no one.

JAMES 1:13 ESV

• •

How are you supposed to forgo a delicious dessert? You love the way the dessert looks so much that it's easy to forget you may not like the way it makes you look later. Before you can make your way to the exit, the last bite of it is in your mouth.

Having to say no to what you personally crave, regardless of what it is, is a herculean feat. As much as you might want to explain away your actions, it was still your decision. Taking personal responsibility is easier said than done, though. It's much less complicated to place the blame on something bigger than yourself.

While that might make you feel better, it doesn't hold up. God will not tempt you. He's not placing urges and inclinations in your head just to see if you will break. Not only that, God always provides a way out of temptations. So the next time you find yourself faced with an unwelcome longing, take joy in the power God gave you to resist it. . .and head toward the exit.

• •

God, I know the things I have to face stem from this fallen world and not from You. I praise You for making my escape route clear.

123

Picture Perfect

For our sake he made him to be sin who knew no sin,
so that in him we might become the righteousness of God.
2 CORINTHIANS 5:21 ESV

. . . .

Many hairdressers receive clients who show them pictures of a celebrity and say, "Make me look like that." During the styling, the hairdresser usually gives a warning that the result most likely won't turn out exactly like the picture. After all, only so much can be done with dye and scissors.

Getting a haircut isn't exactly easy either. Depending on what you're having done, you could potentially be in a chair for hours. Sitting there having to strain your neck or suffering through the pain of bleach on your scalp is not for the faint of heart. However, it is important that you become like that picture. So you continue to sit there and wait, hoping for a miracle.

Just like you won't ever look like that celebrity, your "righteousness" pales in comparison to God's. Jesus is the miracle you need to bridge the gap. Because of His sacrifice, God sees you as holy. Even though you've sinned, you can rejoice that God sees you as one who hasn't. Regardless of what you've done, when you repent, to Him you are picture perfect.

. . . .

God, when I feel like I don't measure up, I thank
You that Your Son made it possible for me to have a
relationship with You. I will delight in Your love.

Don't Forget

"I, even I, am he who blots out your transgressions,
for my own sake, and remembers your sins no more."
ISAIAH 43:25 NIV

Over the years, the principle of "forgive and forget" has morphed into "forgive and never forget." Many people try to walk in forgiveness toward others while secretly clinging to bitter grudges. The idea that you are no longer supposed to recall the offense seems ludicrous. The hurt was deep—how could you ever disregard it?

When a transgression toward you is severe, you have reason to think about it. Forgetting might allow for an identical situation to happen. It is insanity to put yourself in the same predicament and expect something new to happen. The best you can manage is to forgive and love the person. . .with caution.

But even though God is hurt by your sin, He not only forgives but chooses to forget. God's love for you is so immense that nothing is held against you. Once you ask forgiveness and turn from your sin, you can joyfully triumph in the knowledge that what you did is no longer who you are. If you still feel shame when talking to God, don't; He doesn't remember. And of all the things you remember, don't forget: you can still show His love.

Lord, I'm so grateful that You neither recall my sin
nor hold it against me. Please help me forgive myself
so that I can better serve Your kingdom.

Intangible

Remember your word to your servant, for you
have given me hope. My comfort in my suffering
is this: Your promise preserves my life.
PSALM 119:49–50 NIV

When a child is younger, it's acceptable for them to rely on a pacifier, blanket, or a favorite stuffed animal for comfort. But as the years pass, those objects can morph into cigarettes, alcohol, or merely a strong desire for a deep-dish pizza. Adults use these to find some respite from the chaos in a "socially acceptable" way.

It would be nice if we didn't need an outlet to cope with pressure, but stress is inevitable. Eventually, something will happen that'll lead you to seek a way to vent your frustration. . .lest someone end up in jail. If others could be relied on—either to keep their word or not bother you before your morning coffee—then a conduit for anger would be unnecessary.

God can be trusted, and His promises to you are true. If trouble comes, let it come with the joy that God's Word brings to your heart. The comfort His Spirit has for you is better than any blankie or pacifier. Sure, it may be intangible, but you will feel just as safe.

Lord, my hope is in Your loving words to me. I choose to
meditate on them daily so that my joy in You can be full.

Intruder Alert

"So be strong and courageous! Do not be afraid and do not panic before them. For the LORD your God will personally go ahead of you. He will neither fail you nor abandon you."

DEUTERONOMY 31:6 NLT

· ·

There are a number of ways you can protect yourself. Alarm systems can prevent intruders, and weapons can stop a violent act. Bodyguards can keep an individual away from harm or check buildings and cars to make sure their client is secure.

Even with all these avenues, there's no way to completely shield yourself from life. Unforeseen situations will shake up your whole world. Your day-to-day life will become wildly different. There will be no one to warn you—no high-pitched sound to let you know what's ahead. It can't be stopped, and you'll be left dealing with the aftermath.

When your existence leaves you feeling panicked and afraid, know that God is well aware and has seen it all before. You can rejoice knowing that God will never abandon you and that He walks ahead to lead you to safety. No security system or bodyguard can compare to God. With Him, fear can't intrude on your life.

· ·

God, I can feel so scared and insecure sometimes. Thank You for offering Your protection and love amid life's unexpected pain.

It Wasn't Him

Though he brings grief, he will show compassion,
so great is his unfailing love. For he does not
willingly bring affliction or grief to anyone.
LAMENTATIONS 3:32–33 NIV

. . . .

There are now many avenues through which news can quickly spread. But unfortunately, this usually applies only to bad news. If you want to hear good news, you still have to search it out. Witnessing all the destruction that's happening simultaneously can cause you to wonder if God is indeed who He says He is.

Perfect love allows a lot. God's love is so pure that it insists upon free will for everyone. The great benefit to this is that people are more than mindless robots that do and feel only what they are told. The downside is that free will opens the floodgate for countless opportunities to cause great anguish to God, yourself, and others.

But despite anguish's heavy prevalence, God's compassion remains stronger. He doesn't want to watch His creation writhe in pain. He didn't sign off on the dire straits you're in. The joy you need can be found in God's unfailing, unending love. Even when trouble seems ubiquitous, God wasn't the one who caused it.

. . . .

Lord, I won't blame the destruction I see on You. I will instead
look forward to Your glory moving in the midst of it.

New Is Always Better

*"And I will give you a new heart, and I will put a
new spirit in you. I will take out your stony, stubborn
heart and give you a tender, responsive heart."*
Ezekiel 36:26 nlt

. . . .

While many benefits often come with age, most people usually see new as better. New houses, cars, clothes, shoes, and designer purses are enough to brighten anyone's day. And when it comes to food, fresh is definitely preferred.

People often want new material things instead of seeking a fresh perspective or an improved personality. The reason is simple: change is hard. Forcing yourself to be something you are not can seem downright impossible. The perfection you crave eludes you, but it seems to come naturally to others.

No matter how hard you try to embody the traits that you want, you can't do it on your own. All that is good is from God, so if you desire to excel at who you are, He's the one who can help you. You don't have to despair at your inadequacies—you can be joyful that God will help you bridge the gap.

He makes all things new, including you. . .and new is always better.

. . . .

*Lord, please help me become what You want me
to be. I praise You for giving me new life.*

Eye on Others

*Do nothing from selfish ambition or conceit, but
in humility count others more significant than
yourselves. Let each of you look not only to his own
interests, but also to the interests of others.*

PHILIPPIANS 2:3–4 ESV

Self-care is a way to stay mentally, physically, and emotionally well. Before stress wears you down and damages your body, it's vital that you have a plan to manage the pressure. Taking a bubble bath, getting plenty of sleep, praying, and eating well are a few examples of good self-care techniques. Whenever you are whole, you are better able to help others.

But be careful: this important concept can be easily skewed. Addressing your mental state is important, but cutting people out of your life isn't always the answer. Also, ignoring responsibilities due to stress will lead to guilt. Using self-care to avoid life will only lead to heartache.

The reason that self-care often doesn't live up to your expectations is because you were made to look beyond yourself and assist other people. As important and uplifting as personal time is, making sure others have a moment to themselves can fill you with even more joy. God made you to serve and help others. So look after yourself, but also keep an eye on others.

God, help me be mindful of the people around me. Thank You for showing me how to process my stress so that I can bring joy to others.

No Wi-Fi Needed

"Ask and it will be given to you; seek and you will find; knock and the door will be opened to you. For everyone who asks receives; the one who seeks finds; and to the one who knocks, the door will be opened."

MATTHEW 7:7–8 NIV

• •

Because of search engines, the answer to any question lies right at your fingertips. What's the height of Mount Everest? The depth of the Mariana Trench? Five seconds of typing will yield (generally) reliable answers to these questions and many more.

Still, some answers are not so readily available. Searching the internet for ways to navigate a marital dispute can be about as worthwhile as consulting a Magic 8 Ball. It's incredibly frustrating to need a response and be met with silence. Your problems are many, yet your solutions are few.

Fortunately, God promises answers. When you search out who He is, wisdom will follow you. When you are actively walking with God, He will respond to your inquiries. His reply may not be what you expect, but heeding it will bring joy and peace. So when you seek, knock, and ask, you can anticipate His answer.

Even better, you don't need Wi-Fi with God.

• •

Lord, I will choose to call on You in every uncertainty.
I ask for Your wisdom and guidance when I am
faced with what I do not comprehend.

Exponentially

Why, my soul, are you downcast? Why so disturbed
within me? Put your hope in God, for I will
yet praise him, my Savior and my God.
PSALM 42:11 NIV

• •

You know exactly why you feel hopeless—nobody has to tell you. And
anyone who talks to you for longer than five minutes knows it too. The
disconnect you feel is so great that it keeps you from living. All your
attention is devoted to the pain from your problem. You'd jump at the
chance to get rid of it, but no such opportunities arise.

These dismal feelings can actually be addicting. Contentment starts
feeling weird because it is so unfamiliar to you. Feelings are supposed
to be fleeting, but yours seem to stick around. Anxiousness and worry
are like guests who've overstayed their welcome, but if they finally do
leave, you're almost sad about it.

Regardless of your emotions, praising God is still an option. Your
goal is not to ignore what you're feeling but to praise God in the midst
of it. Your hope is in God, and once you express that, your joy will
increase—exponentially.

• •

Father God, help me not to be addicted to obstructive emotions.
Whenever my feelings overwhelm me, I will acknowledge them
while still choosing to experience the glory of Your presence.

Truth

From the fruit of their lips people are filled with good things, and the work of their hands brings them reward.

PROVERBS 12:14 NIV

. . . .

If people were honest when asked if they'd prefer to hear gossip or the truth, their answer might surprise you. People often desire truth for its ability to give a clear direction even in crisis, but gossip can create a bond between people. Gossip produces an inherent sense of superiority. Even though we all know dishing dirt on others is wrong, it's easy to resort to when we need to feel better about ourselves.

As easy as it is to talk about others, speaking poorly about ourselves can go just as smoothly. The thoughts we have about ourselves are worse than the whispers we make about other people—and they're not even emotionally rewarding. Telling ourselves we are lazy and incompetent doesn't feel nearly as good as saying our neighbors are.

The Bible makes it clear that your aim should be truth—not only about those around you but about yourself. Lies don't last, but truth will. If you speak good things, you'll also have joy in the respect you receive from those around you.

Gossip can be entertaining, but the truth is far more fun.

. . . .

Lord, thank You for helping me manage the words I speak concerning myself and others. I choose to speak with the veracity of Your love.

133

Claimed

*Dear friends, now we are children of God, and
what we will be has not yet been made known.
But we know that when Christ appears, we shall
be like him, for we shall see him as he is.*

1 JOHN 3:2 NIV

No matter which way you slice it, you've been forsaken. Everyone you thought you could call on is no longer there. The isolation you feel is as tangible as the phone in your hand. Even the words *mother* and *father* find no audience when they leave your mouth.

When Jesus was betrayed by Judas, everything He had was taken away. As He hung on the cross, the soldiers cast lots for His belongings. Every status He possessed—even the title of carpenter—was stripped from Him. It didn't matter who He had been or who His mother and Father were—in that moment, He was nothing.

The suffering that Christ endured allows you to have all that He lost during His sacrifice. Your lineage no longer matters—you are now a child of God. The clothing you wear is His mercy and grace. Your joy no longer lies in your achievements but in the fact that God claims you as His own.

*Father God, thank You for healing the pain I feel
from abandonment. I believe that because of the
sacrifice You made, I will lack nothing.*

Lackluster

*Looking to Jesus, the founder and perfecter of
our faith, who for the joy that was set before him
endured the cross, despising the shame, and is
seated at the right hand of the throne of God.*

HEBREWS 12:2 ESV

When animals get distracted by shiny objects or squirrels, it's adorable, cute, and funny. But when humans get distracted, they're labeled as self-absorbed. When you're not able to focus on the duties at hand, life slowly starts to fall apart.

The reason it can be hard to direct your attention is because it is difficult to aim at a moving target. There are too many options that all come at a different price. Your stamina is waning, and you aren't sure where to place your faith.

When you look to Jesus, He will perfect your faith. Jesus endured much so that you too could be seated at the right hand of God. . .and He did it joyfully. Living is extremely difficult, and bravery can be hard to come by. That's why you must remember the joy in store for you—not only in heaven but here on earth. When you are a part of God's kingdom, the jewels of this world seem lackluster in comparison.

*Lord, You are the best distraction. I will keep my sights
on You instead of shame and guilt, and I will embrace the
delights You have for now. . .as well as in heaven.*

Scars

He heals the brokenhearted
and binds up their wounds.
PSALM 147:3 NIV

· ·

If you don't clean a wound, it can become worse. The body is amazing at rebuilding itself, but it sometimes requires help. If the cut is deep enough, leaving it to mend on its own is not an option. Ointment, bandages, or perhaps even stitches are required to restore the broken area. Eventually, the covering is removed and you are whole.

Unfortunately, there's no store that sells a salve for a broken heart. It would be nice if you could reach in and glue a shattered heart back together, but that isn't possible. On top of the immense pain you are feeling, you also feel alone in patching it back together. But leaving yourself to treat your own trauma could make it worse.

God does not leave you alone in your suffering. He is with you to comfort you—that's why He sent the Holy Spirit. But He does more than just stand beside you: He will do what is necessary to completely heal your heart and mind. You can have joy in giving your hurt to God because He knows what to do. Doctors might fix a wound, but only God can heal scars.

· ·

Lord, I trust You with my deep suffering. I know Your love
will take away these scars and make me brand-new.

Perfect Pace

"The LORD himself goes before you and will be with you; he will never leave you nor forsake you. Do not be afraid; do not be discouraged."

Sloths are known for their sluggishness. They move so slowly that it can take them all day to go from one spot on a tree to another. They sleep quite a bit, and even when they're threatened, they only move about a foot a minute. Cheetahs, however, are known for their speed. They can run fifty to eighty miles per hour. When the cheetah springs into action, its prey's fate is practically sealed.

Have you ever felt like either of these mammals? Some days, you just want to wait a tough situation out; others, you may swing in like a wrecking ball and attack the issue with zeal. If the option you chose matches the predicament, you feel accomplished. But if you chose wrong, you might feel exhausted or fearful.

Belonging to God means He takes care of you by going before you. When you follow His strides, you won't be left feeling tired or anxious but delighted in His guidance. There's no need to lag behind or rush ahead when God directs your steps. His pace is perfect.

Lord, help me keep in time with Your steps. I give my fear and anxiety to You so that I can promptly fulfill Your will.

Bless

Show hospitality to one another without grumbling.
As each has received a gift, use it to serve one
another, as good stewards of God's varied grace.
1 Peter 4:9–10 esv

. . . .

Milena sat, wondering how to help. It was clear that everyone knew exactly what to do. . .except her. Everything she could think of was already being taken care of. Milena had a knack for home-baked goods, so despite food already being prepared, she decided to make her famous apple cake. Later, she would find out how important her contribution had been.

Finding your talent might not be as simple as baking a cake. Certain things you like, such as playing the piano, may only lead to stress. Finding the place where passion meets understanding is no small feat. This becomes even harder if your loved ones confirm there's nothing special about you.

The Bible is there to remind you that not only are you special to God, He gave you a gift. You can be joyful that God doesn't place desires in your heart without reason. When you spend time with Him, your affections will reveal your purpose. It may not be baking or playing the piano, but it will bless others just the same.

. . . .

Father God, reveal to me the gifts You've given me. Help
me use them to bring others joy and draw them to You.

I Like Life

*I remain confident of this: I will see the goodness of
the LORD in the land of the living. Wait for the LORD;
be strong and take heart and wait for the LORD.*
PSALM 27:13–14 NIV

- -

If hope were a human, you would want him closer than even a best
friend. All your free time would be spent making more memories with
him. If you were just going about your day, you'd want to know what
he was thinking. Whenever a situation arose, you'd insist upon his
knowledge and viewpoint. Being with him would be a perpetual spree.

If life were a person, however, you'd most likely want to punch him.
He'd only seem to radiate negativity. Whenever you would attempt to
look on the bright side, all he'd show you would be the dark corners.
Trying to be positive around him would fall flat and leave you feeling
hollow.

Walking with God may make you view life in a different way. Regardless of what life might be telling you, your confidence can remain
in God. When life starts emphasizing all your woes, you can rejoice
knowing you will see God's righteousness come to pass. Waiting on
God's goodness will not leave you disappointed—you may even find
yourself *liking* life!

- -

*Father God, I trust Your sovereignty and pure love for me. You relate
to my feelings, and I know things will turn out just as they should be.*

He Loves You for You

"I now realize how true it is that God does not show favoritism but accepts from every nation the one who fears him and does what is right."
ACTS 10:34–35 NIV

. . . .

Nothing about being a female is easy. In fact, there's been a loud cry insisting upon an easier existence. Instead of being marginalized, women should be celebrated. Submissiveness should no longer be desirable—assertiveness should be developed instead. And don't get them started on the pressing beauty standards that turn each holiday or event into a demand for weight loss.

It would be amazing if others considered not gender but merit and ability. The number of times you've been overlooked, frowned upon, or told to stay calm has left a sour taste in your mouth. It's also hard to feel safe when others make you feel like an easy target.

Jesus didn't stigmatize women—He included and empowered them in a culture that did not. The God you serve does not care about gender—He only cares if you love Him. When you love someone, you want to do right by that person, not cause that person pain. You can have complete joy in the truth that God loves you for you. . .and that He overlooks what society tells you to focus on.

. . . .

Lord, thank You for hearing and seeing who I really am.
Help me share with others the joy of Your unbiased love.

Burden-Free

*"Martha, Martha," the Lord answered, "you are
worried and upset about many things, but few things
are needed—or indeed only one. Mary has chosen what
is better, and it will not be taken away from her."*

LUKE 10:41–42 NIV

• •

Martha was the original "Hostess with the Mostess." When she heard that Jesus and His disciples were in town, she opened her home to them. In the midst of preparation, Jesus began to teach, and Martha noticed her sister, Mary, was at His feet listening. Martha immediately asked Jesus to rectify the situation. Instead, His response emancipated not only Martha but other women as well.

When Mary sat at Jesus' feet, it was not just controversial—it was countercultural. Women were not disciples. Martha knew this, so she asked for Jesus to correct Mary because she probably didn't want to hear about it later. When Martha heard that Jesus approved of Mary's actions, she didn't feel admonished—she felt liberated.

God has untethered you from everything, even your preconceived ideas of societal norms. You can experience overflowing joy because Jesus wants you to sit at His feet. He wants you as His disciple. Completing your duties is not a prerequisite for following Him. Following Jesus is burden-free.

• •

*Lord, when I feel oppressed, even by my own doing, I thank
You for giving me freedom. I will stop looking at what
culture says and embrace Your countercultural love.*

Home

*"There are many rooms in My Father's house.
If it were not so, I would have told you. I am
going away to make a place for you."*

JOHN 14:2 NLV

. . . .

Hearing a knock on the door, especially when the only person you were planning on entertaining that evening was yourself, is off-putting. There's no time to plan anything, and you're pretty sure your food supply consists primarily of pickles and crackers. A bit of preparation could've led to a fun night, but now you might end up just staring at each other. How boring. And awkward.

Even if you have an address, you can still sometimes feel like an unexpected visitor in your own residence. Nothing seems quite right to you. Everything around you just doesn't fit. It's the same when you go to other places as well, which is discouraging.

Jesus said His Father's house had many rooms, but what is even more interesting is that Jesus said He is going to make a place for you. Not some cookie-cutter hotel room, but a room perfectly crafted to suit you. Spending time with the Holy Spirit and getting a glimpse of the kingdom you belong to will fill you with a joy that a worldly home cannot.

. . . .

*Father God, I know You've prepared a place for me to be with You.
Until I get there, I will revel in glimpses I get because of Your love.*

Spring Forth

"Before I formed you in the womb I knew
you, before you were born I set you apart;
I appointed you as a prophet to the nations."

JEREMIAH 1:5 NIV

. . . .

Shiphrah and Puah were midwives to the Hebrew women, and Pharaoh petitioned them to execute all males because he wanted to keep the Hebrew population down. But the midwives feared God, so in response to Pharaoh's orders, they said the Hebrew women were so lively and vigorous that they delivered the baby before they arrived. In doing so, they prevented a genocide, and the Lord blessed Shiphrah and Puah with a great dynasty.

It can be tempting to confine yourself to your culture's rules to avoid resistance. But in time, you start to realize how suffocating this box is. There has to be more to life than keeping up with the opinions espoused by television, social media, or your friend group.

God formed you in your mother's womb, and that was the last place you were meant to be enclosed. God never intended for you to be boxed in, as He will not be boxed in by anyone. Rejoice in your purpose and calling and, just like Shiphrah and Puah, watch as new life springs forth.

. . . .

Lord, I believe You have a calling on my life. The pressures that
others place upon me can't diminish what You will do through me.

Raised

*Indeed, we felt that we had received the sentence
of death. But that was to make us rely not on
ourselves but on God who raises the dead.*

2 CORINTHIANS 1:9 ESV

It's been awhile since you've been to church, and the idea of going back
does not appeal to you. Even though you've confronted your sin and
repented, the people you love still judge you. While you know God's
love has made you whole, people treat you like you're tainted. You feel
completely shut out from the group you once loved.

Their whispers about you are louder than they know. Even though
you've attempted to let it go, it still makes your stomach twinge with
guilt. It would be nice to reintroduce yourself, but they've embraced the
reputation they've created for you. The thought of attending somewhere
else has crossed your mind.

There's no need to search for belonging, because you have it in
Jesus. You can hold your head high and rejoice in God, who loves to
restore. As flawed as you may be, God will redeem you and silence
those whispers. Being ostracized may feel like a death sentence, but
God is known for raising the dead.

*Lord, I will not let others dictate my worth. I praise You for
Your sacrifice that enables me to live without shame.*

Jesus Isn't Magic

From now on let no one cause me trouble,
for I bear on my body the marks of Jesus.
GALATIANS 6:17 ESV

. . . .

When trouble strikes, many people turn to a variety of sources for help. Phone calls are made, seers are consulted, and tarot cards are used. For a fleeting moment, they feel a sense of control, but then reality sets in with a vengeance.

There's no herb or crystal that can keep trouble from happening in your life. When the money isn't there to pay a bill, when you get a flat tire on your way to work, or when your health fails you, no charm can halt the inevitable. Life's circumstances can't be reversed, and no fortune-teller can ward off the unexpected.

Belonging to Jesus doesn't mean you won't face anxiety and worry. But it does mean that because of Jesus' ultimate sacrifice, you have the authority to treat things that aren't as though they were. Believing that God will move in a situation empowers you to revel in the unexpected joy that follows. Jesus isn't magic, and His answers are no illusion.

. . . .

Lord, I understand that because I've been marked
by You, trouble has less of an effect on me. I will
follow You and wait in joyful anticipation.

Found

Where shall I go from your Spirit?
Or where shall I flee from your presence?
PSALM 139:7 ESV

When you played hide-and-seek as a child, you probably had more fun in hiding than in being the seeker. You spent all your energy trying not to laugh as the seeker drew closer. If you could maintain your composure, you might've even outlasted all the others and won the round. It filled you with pride to be considered the best hider.

While this game is still fun as an adult, concealing who you are can turn into a chore. Grappling with sin is not something you can always do alone. It takes vulnerability to obtain healing. Your first instinct might be to run away from God because He is holy and you are not.

Not only is it impossible to hide from God, there's absolutely no reason to do so. He has seen and heard it all, so nothing makes Him blush. Let the knowledge that God is aware of you bring you peace, and let His presence bring unequivocal joy. No matter how good your hiding spot, God can find you there. And with Him, the fun is in being found.

Father God, I want my knowledge of Your existence to turn into experiencing Your presence. I will not let my guilt or shame hinder my relationship with You. I will repent and draw closer.

Wildest Dreams

Now all glory to God, who is able, through his mighty power at work within us, to accomplish infinitely more than we might ask or think. Glory to him in the church and in Christ Jesus through all generations forever and ever! Amen.
EPHESIANS 3:20–21 NLT

Looking at your friends' vacation pictures may make you want to plan one for yourself. Seeing the hotel rooms and plates of food, you find yourself wishing that you could live that way daily. You wish all your friends and family could enjoy that type of lifestyle as well.

But just like having Christmas every day would diminish its grandeur, living in a perpetual vacation would lose its appeal. Pointless fights would still break out, and no amount of coffee could soothe your nerves. No matter how clear the water or how warm the fire, you'd soon want out. It's a lovely fantasy, but it doesn't translate to reality.

The things that you dream of and desire cannot hold a candle to what God can manifest in your life. He's not bound or limited in His ways. When you allow the Holy Spirit to align you with God's will, the results will be better than anything in your wildest dreams.

Lord, I don't want to settle for less than what You're able to do in my life. I will have joy in giving You all the glory for what I am given.

Gott Ist Deine Freude

Do not be full of joy when the one who hates you
falls. Do not let your heart be glad when he trips.
The Lord will see it and will not be pleased, and
He will turn away His anger from him.
PROVERBS 24:17–18 NLV

. . . .

While you may not speak German, there is a word in the German language that may ring true for you: *Schadenfreude.* This word encapsulates the feeling of delight you have when an enemy experiences misfortune. Even if you can't say it, you've most likely felt it.

The opposite of Schadenfreude is *Mitfreude*—the shared joy you experience at others' good fortune. This emotion is slightly harder to achieve. It's more satisfying to watch the downfall of someone who has hurt you than to be elated when someone else meets prosperity.

Reveling in another's undoing means that person holds power over you—and that's not what God wants. He cares for you too much, and He'll do all He can to protect your heart. If you are feigning happiness for someone because you feel like it should be your turn, you are limiting the infinite goodness of God.

But if the German language still interests you, here's one more phrase to remember: *Gott ist deine freude*—"God is my joy."

. . . .

Lord, my triumph and elation are in You. Help
me be gracious when my enemy is broken, and help
me rejoice each time You show Your mercy.

A Whisper Away

*Then a great and powerful wind tore the mountains
apart and shattered the rocks before the LORD, but the
LORD was not in the wind. After the wind there was
an earthquake, but the LORD was not in the earthquake.
After the earthquake came a fire, but the LORD was not
in the fire. And after the fire came a gentle whisper.*

1 KINGS 19:11–12 NIV

Anyone, if given the opportunity, would push the big red button to
explode a building that was planned for demolition. There's something
amazing about hearing the huge boom and watching as the structure
crumbles to the ground. Feeling the vibrations flow through you gives
the undeniable impression that something substantial has just happened.

When Elijah found himself in a cave hiding in fear for his life,
he needed God to show up in a great way. He thought God would be
in the roaring wind, earthquake, and crackling fire, but He wasn't: the
Lord came in a gentle whisper.

It is wonderful when God moves in resounding ways, but He is
still in the quiet too, and you can take bliss in the stillness. When you
spend time quietly listening to His Spirit, His peace can shake you
more significantly than any explosive. God is powerful, but He's also
just a whisper away.

*God, while I want You to use Your mighty hand to right
all wrongs, I will follow Your soft tug upon my heart.*

Liberated

He has delivered us from the domain of darkness and
transferred us to the kingdom of his beloved Son,
in whom we have redemption, the forgiveness of sins.
COLOSSIANS 1:13–14 ESV

Some people will do just about anything to escape reality. Whether it's scrolling our phones, getting lost in a book, jumping from hobby to hobby, watching a movie, or even taking a vacation, we humans love just checking out for a while. These occasional tune-out sessions leave us feeling refreshed.

Some things, however, you can't run away from. No amount of scrolling will relieve your pain. No piece of literature will teleport you to a better reality. And absolutely no hobby will fill the void inside your soul.

Real life can weigh you down and cause you to become jaded and analytical, but God has so much more in store for you. His kingdom is available for you to abide in. Don't be consumed with what you are faced with; rather, believe with joy that you have been delivered.

Trying to escape isn't necessary when you've been liberated.

God, it is easy to get stuck in the routine of this
world. Help me live at the higher standard You call
me to so that I can bring glory to Your name.

"Some People"?

"How can you say to your brother, 'Let me take the speck out of your eye,' when all the time there is a plank in your own eye? You hypocrite, first take the plank out of your own eye, and then you will see clearly to remove the speck from your brother's eye."

MATTHEW 7:4–5 NIV

· ·

If we could get paid for the judgments we make about others, most of us would be able to purchase our dream car—with cash. It's not something we set out to do; it happens spontaneously when presented with something we find unfavorable. We know we aren't perfect, but "some people" have serious issues.

Seeing fault in others can delay confronting the imperfections in ourselves. Everything that could be improved in us has a great explanation for why it hasn't. We use our circumstances, emotional stress, and feelings of being misunderstood as excuses to disregard the areas we need to grow in.

Just like removing an eyelash from your eye makes it feel better, you will improve when you recognize your faults. This is meant not to bring shame but to provide joy at the prospect of redemption. Let God heal you first so that you can help others with impaired vision.

· ·

Lord, I have issues, just like everyone else. Make me a vessel of Your grace while You work on me and others.

Speak with God

"But when you pray, go away by yourself, shut the door behind you, and pray to your Father in private. Then your Father, who sees everything, will reward you."

MATTHEW 6:6 NLT

If the act of talking to yourself might land you in a psychiatric ward, how are you supposed to feel when you pray? It can feel odd to speak to what you can't see. You know that the ultimate goal is to draw closer to God, but you don't know how to get nearer to what you don't understand.

During your day, you may talk to several people you don't know, such as a barista or someone jogging down your street. If you were to continue to see these people and say more than hello, you would eventually learn more about them. With more one-on-one conversations, you might even wind up calling them your friend.

Prayer is having a conversation with God. You may not understand Him fully, but He knows Himself really well. God will tell you all you need to understand. The closer you are to God, the more your joy and appreciation for Him will increase.

If it's not unnatural to chat with someone new, you don't need to feel awkward speaking with God.

Lord, please reveal to me more about Yourself. I don't want our relationship to be one-sided. And since You created me, help me understand who You are so that our joy can be full.

Inconceivable

*The reason the Son of God appeared was
to destroy the works of the devil.*
1 JOHN 3:8 ESV

. . . .

Horrific. Tragic. Appalling. When a terrible event occurs, these words often appear on the news and across social media, even though they fail to convey the actual depth of pain and despair involved. As you hear them, you start to wonder why things like this happen. . .and if they could possibly be a sign of God's punishment.

There is only one who has come to steal, kill, and destroy—and it is not the Savior. Jesus came to unravel and dissolve the enemy's plans. When you witness death and destruction, you can rest assured it didn't happen because God struck His gavel. Just because you can't find an answer doesn't mean God had something to do with it.

When God casts judgment, it looks like the Savior on a cross, shedding His blood so that you could feel the joy of being redeemed and reconciled back to Him. The Lord isn't a stern master monitoring your every move—He's a devoted Father. The mercy of the Lord is great, and His love is inconceivable.

. . . .

*Father God, You offer hope and restoration, not despair and
agony. Even when I don't know why something has happened,
I will embrace Your love and not look for judgment.*

153

Eternity Won't Be Enough

So Christ was sacrificed once to take away the sins of many; and he will appear a second time, not to bear sin, but to bring salvation to those who are waiting for him.

HEBREWS 9:28 NIV

. . . .

Attempting to pick up something that's too heavy can send you to the chiropractor. As much as you might want it out of your way, it is worth waiting for another person's help. You are impatient, though, and as you go to pick it up, you end up on the floor with it.

If your sin were an object, carrying it would be impossible. It would be too heavy and cumbersome to move. Even though transgressions aren't tangible objects, they can still feel overwhelming. When you sin, the burden can be so great that it crushes you.

The reason you can't bear your sin is because you were not meant to. When sin came into the world, the only one who could endure it was Christ. He will then return a second time for those awaiting salvation. You can be joyful that Christ has not only put away your sin but that He is coming back for you. When Christ does return, the eternity you get to spend with Him won't be enough.

. . . .

Lord, thank You for loving me enough to do what I could not.
I will start praising You now so that I can get a glimpse of heaven.

Sting

And so let us come near to God with a true heart full of faith. Our hearts must be made clean from guilty feelings and our bodies washed with pure water.

HEBREWS 10:22 NLV

Denial can be a useful tool. It sometimes provides the time needed to digest alarming information. By allowing a moment to breathe, the situation might be handled better—and with fewer possible regrets. An immediate overreaction could exacerbate the problem.

Most of the time, however, denial is not helpful. If you were to see a Lego on the floor and pretend it didn't exist, the agony you'd feel later after stepping on it barefoot would jolt you back to reality. Trying to process information that your brain wants to ignore can end up being painful and difficult.

Jesus can only accept what you do. If you are in despair but try to pretend that you're not, you're saying that Jesus can't be trusted with that. There's no need to attempt to save face when you are talking with Him. When you admit your struggle, you can be filled with relief and joy that He will bring you through. When you are authentic in your anguish and trust God with it, it no longer holds the sting it once did.

Lord, I will no longer hide the way I feel in hopes that my emotions will just go away. I will give them all to You because in You alone I trust.

Miracles Happen

Jesus looked at them and said, "With man it is impossible,
but not with God. For all things are possible with God."
MARK 10:27 ESV

• •

Five miles down, at the bottom of the ocean, lives the Mariana snailfish. The amount of pressure this fish endures would obliterate other animals. However, its rubbery bones allow the fish to thrive where others cannot.

Most of us, however, aren't born with the ability to flourish under duress. Perhaps the weight of life seems to be crushing you slowly. You've become acutely aware of your own fragility. When others tell you that you can do it—that you're stronger than you know—it is difficult to believe.

The reason it's hard to accept what they say is because it is not true. When you are met with an impossible situation, you *can't* do it. You know exactly how much strength you have—not much.

Those facts are irrelevant, though. When God gets involved, nothing is out of your reach. The power to change reality begins with prayer, not sheer will or determination. If it would take a miracle to bring you peace and joy, that's okay—with God, those happen every day!

• •

God, I will not focus on the limitations I see.
I will direct my attention toward the glory You
will receive when a miracle comes to pass.

Rumors

By this you know the Spirit of God: every spirit that
confesses that Jesus Christ has come in the flesh is from God,
and every spirit that does not confess Jesus is not from God.
1 JOHN 4:2–3 ESV

Rumors can cause serious damage and possibly even destroy a reputation. Depending on the rumor's gravity, you may never view that person the same way again. Relationships may be irreparably wrecked, which is why it is important to verify what you are told.

How you view God is pivotal to your walk with Him. The depth of your relationship is based on how good you perceive Him to be. When horrendous events happen, some will come out of the woodwork and give their two cents about where they think God stands in the matter.

Jesus was the exact, perfect representation of God, and He died to save you. If you come across an opinion (or spirit) that Jesus is not the Son of God and did not defeat hell, death, and the grave, you can disregard it. Jesus' resurrection changed the course of history. Your joy can remain steadfast because His purpose is life and redemption. Remember to actively seek God out. . .and don't believe everything you hear.

Father God, thank You for the guidance and truth
of the Holy Spirit. Help me know You intimately so
that I may better represent Your loving heart.

Memory

I call as my heart grows faint; lead me to the rock that is higher than I. For you have been my refuge, a strong tower against the foe.

PSALM 61:2–3 NIV

If a house is on fire but there's still time to grab a few things, memories are often the first to be saved. They cannot be replaced. As horrible as this tragedy is, the blow is lessened when these items are spared.

When you feel like you're the house on fire, though, all you're able to see is destruction. The things you once enjoyed don't mean as much to you anymore. You're using all of your brain power to try to figure out a way to escape this circumstance. The last thing you feel like doing is remembering the good things.

But God has been, and will continue to be, your refuge. Given enough time, you could probably create a huge list of every occasion in which God has come through for you. Take heart and be joyful because today is no different. God doesn't come through for you once and then stop there—He will continue to prevail and make wonderful memories with you.

God, even though it is hard to recall because of my pain, I know that You've been there for me—and that You won't stop today.

Renovate

We break down every thought and proud thing that puts itself up against the wisdom of God. We take hold of every thought and make it obey Christ.

2 Corinthians 10:5 NLV

• •

If all your dire thoughts about the state of the world came true, the results would be worse than any dystopian sci-fi novel. If you managed to stay safe from violent people, the elements would end up overcoming you anyway. There would be no hiding from chaos and death.

If the unspeakable thoughts you had about yourself were reflected in a mirror, you'd be terrified. Every reflective surface would be shrouded by a blanket, distorting your image. Everywhere you went, you'd expect to be accompanied by sorrowful organ music.

The only thing that can change the postapocalyptic landscape inside your head is the Word of God. He made you in His image. When you hide God's Word in your heart, you have something to guard against intrusive ideas. The joy that comes from being able to cast down vain imaginations is priceless. If you don't like the place your thoughts carry you, let wisdom renovate your mind.

• •

Lord, I thank You that I don't have to deal with my imagination on my own. Let Your Word take hold of any foolishness and Your wisdom restore my joy and peace.

Yes!

"His master said to him, 'Well done, good and faithful servant. You have been faithful over a little; I will set you over much. Enter into the joy of your master.'"
MATTHEW 25:23 ESV

· ·

Parents love seeing straight As on their child's report card. It lets them know they are doing well. The fact that their child is flourishing means a great deal to them. They start eagerly bragging to their friends about the accomplishment, unable to suppress a grin.

If you brought home a "life" report card today, what grades would you find? Would it be full of Fs? Would you be shocked to find that life is a test you didn't study for? Maybe others around you seemed to understand the assignment, but you somehow missed it. Given how many hoops you're expected to jump through, it seems like no one wants you to succeed.

God wants great success for you. He has given you so much, and He can't wait to give you even more. God sees your faithfulness, especially on the hard days, and wants you to know that joy is coming. You don't ever have to wonder if God has victories planned for you—the answer to that question will always be yes!

· ·

Father God, I want to deepen my faith in You. Help me achieve Your plan for my life—I want only to be accomplished in Your eyes.

Ice Cream

*Perfume and incense bring joy to the heart, and the
pleasantness of a friend springs from their heartfelt advice.*

PROVERBS 27:9 NIV

When something exciting happens to you, you immediately want to
tell your best friends. The happiness they have for you will be the cherry
on top of an already great day. Before you pick up the phone to tell
them, you think of a place you all can go to celebrate—that ice cream
shop down the street sounds perfect!

Some of your "friends," however, don't always smile for you. When
you share information, they give a flat "huh, that's great." You can be
bursting with a fantastic idea or incredible news, and then they just
rip the rug right out from beneath you. Talking with them makes you
feel completely deflated. All you wanted was for them to share in your
happiness, but now you've lost your own joy too.

It's vital to pick the right person to confide in. God made you to
be relational, and the person you choose to interact with on a consis-
tent basis affects you. God wants you to show care and love toward
everyone, but the Bible also speaks of a friend that sticks closer than
a brother.

Having a friend like that is sweeter than ice cream.

*Lord, thank You for healing me of the wounds of deficient
relationships. Help me to not only be a good friend
but to nurture the friendships You've given me.*

No Substitutes

And behold, the star that they had seen when it rose went before them until it came to rest over the place where the child was. When they saw the star, they rejoiced exceedingly with great joy.

MATTHEW 2:9–10 ESV

· ·

Emilia-Romagna is a historical region in Italy that produces *parmigiano reggiano*, better known as parmesan cheese. According to the European Union and United States laws, Emilia-Romagna is the only place that parmigiano reggiano can be produced. All other parmesan cheeses are imitations.

There's only one source of joy, but substitutes exist everywhere. Driving down the road, you'll see several businesses claiming to have what you need. The radio will advertise the latest natural supplement to boost your serotonin. And as you scroll on your phone, several articles will promise to show you how to find joy in daily life. But none of these suggestions will last. These knockoffs only bring you fleeting happiness.

True joy comes from only one place, and the wise men knew that. They followed the star with great delight because they knew it would lead to their ultimate joy. There's no reason to settle for happiness, which can fade so quickly. Jesus is your source of joy—accept no substitute.

· ·

Father God, I've been pacified by happiness when all I need is Your lasting joy. Let Your joy overflow in me, and let it flow through me to others.

Spoonful of Joy

A joyful heart is good medicine, but a
crushed spirit dries up the bones.
PROVERBS 17:22 ESV

. . . .

Aloe vera has many restorative properties. It can improve digestive health and even aid with acne. But out of all the things the versatile gel can do, it is best known for its ability to heal burns. If a sunburn makes you regret that day at the beach, aloe vera will have you back in the ocean in no time.

Some burns require a lot more than an icy cold gel, however. When a relationship goes up in smoke, it's hard to find something to remove the sting. When you experience the painful "ouch" of touching on a hot topic with a friend, you're unlikely to walk away unscathed. The only solution you see is to return to your bed and nurse your wounds.

Just like aloe vera, God's endless well of joy can soothe you when life leaves you feeling hot and parched. Joy is the medicine you need to get out of your proverbial bed. If a spoonful of sugar can help medicine go down, joy will certainly make life less bitter.

. . . .

God, I don't want to become embittered and resentful at my life.
I will be grateful for Your blessings. My joy is secure in You.

Admit It!

But he was pierced for our transgressions; he was crushed for our iniquities; upon him was the chastisement that brought us peace, and with his wounds we are healed.

ISAIAH 53:5 ESV

. . . .

If you grew up with siblings and your parents caught you doing something wrong, the finger-pointing would commence. A symphony of "She did it!" or "It's his fault" would break out. Ethics went out the window as long as you weren't the one who ended up in trouble. In fact, seeing your annoying sibling get the blame made your day.

Sadly, blame-shifting doesn't disappear with age. The humiliation of a misdeed is so great that it becomes unbearable. People go to great lengths to try lessening the blow of the consequence. Everyone wants to be perceived as humble, but no one likes being humbled.

Thankfully, Jesus took the blame for you. When He stood before the Father, He bore the weight of all sin. There's no need to let guilt and shame follow you—all that remains is the mercy and goodness of the Lord. When you do sin, hold on to joy because there is a way out. Because of the magnitude of what Jesus did on the cross, admitting and turning from sin will bring peace.

. . . .

Father God, confessing my transgressions is difficult and painful. However, I will admit them to You. I know Your truth and love will set me free.

Monotonous

Christ made everything in the heavens and on the earth. He made everything that is seen and things that are not seen. He made all the powers of heaven. Everything was made by Him and for Him.

COLOSSIANS 1:16 NLV

It doesn't matter that you've seen it a thousand times—you are in the middle of rewatching your favorite television show. With its familiarity comes so much comfort. You can quote every episode and incorporate those jokes into your daily life. After a long day, you can always unwind by laughing at the characters in the show.

Not everything you get to repeat is entertaining, though. The everyday grind of the workforce can get exhausting. The never-ending loads of laundry can have you questioning your sanity. And don't even mention that perpetual mess in the kitchen.

Jesus fed people, washed others' feet, and insisted that the little children be able to run to Him. The God who made everything, even what you cannot see, chose to experience the mundane. Jesus used the humdrum of daily life to serve others.

When life gets monotonous, serve like He did—joy will be next to you.

Lord, doing the same task over and over gets tedious. Help me do each task as unto You, and let me find the joy You have for me in it.

If the Shoe Fits

Now may the God of peace make you holy in every way,
and may your whole spirit and soul and body be kept
blameless until our Lord Jesus Christ comes again.

1 Thessalonians 5:23 NLT

There's a reason the word *chopsticks* is almost always plural—using only one chopstick would leave you hungry. Likewise, you can't make much of a sweater with only one needle. And imagine if you only had one shoe! One foot would always be in pain.

People can spend their entire lives looking for what completes them. They walk around feeling detached and sullen. This search seems to be never-ending. While they want to be useful, they don't feel like they are enough. Only having half of something makes it difficult to use.

Jesus rescued all of you when He went to the cross. The Bible says He can restore your whole spirit, soul, and body. You are not half of anything; rather, you can have joy because Jesus made you complete in Him. With God, there is no lack. If you are missing anything, it's spending more time with Jesus.

That is a shoe that will definitely fit!

God, help me prioritize spending time with Your
Holy Spirit. I don't want to waste time looking
for what is already found in Your presence.

No Regrets

*Instead, we will speak the truth in love, growing
in every way more and more like Christ,
who is the head of his body, the church.*
EPHESIANS 4:15 NLT

Following your truth is an ideology that focuses on authenticity. It's meant to enable you to make choices that reflect who you are. If something doesn't line up with your core values, you can walk away from it without needing to feel guilty.

Sounds great, right? Well, not exactly. Such freedom to do what you want will only end up enslaving you. What feels good soon starts replacing the ultimate truth of God.

What you feel is true doesn't matter—it's all about what God says is true. Every day, your faith draws you to the life-changing love of God. The things you want to be true don't matter when compared to what He sacrificed for you. When the veracity of God's love envelops you, you'll have no choice but to share it with others, which will also increase your joy.

Follow God's truth and rejoice in it—you won't regret it.

*Lord, there are so many things I would love to be
true. Help me weigh my untrustworthy heart against
Your truth so that I can serve You better.*

Renovate

You yourselves like living stones are being built up as a spiritual house, to be a holy priesthood, to offer spiritual sacrifices acceptable to God through Jesus Christ.

1 PETER 2:5 ESV

How you decorate your home tells a lot about who you are. People tend to surround themselves with what makes them comfortable. From shabby chic to contemporary, there's a style out there to suit everyone. If you lived in a space you hated, you'd eventually find yourself wanting to redo all of it.

Sometimes, life throws you into undesirable places. The building doesn't matter so much—it's the way you feel. Trying to tell yourself that you're where you want to be is pointless. It feels like you're walking in the dark and stubbing your toe on everything.

God created you to be a spiritual house. When you worship Him as well as study and live out His Word, you become furnished with the fruits of the Spirit. Your location takes second place to the God you serve and love. Rejoice in the Lord while He works on you and renovates your life. Shiplap might go out of style, but the work God does through you is timeless.

Lord, I will come to You singing praises and worshipping Your holy name. I want to partner with You and glorify You with who I am.

168

Heal People

Confess your sins to each other and pray for each other so that you may be healed. The earnest prayer of a righteous person has great power and produces wonderful results.

JAMES 5:16 NLT

• •

When you are on a flight, the obligatory safety protocol explains that in an emergency, you are to put the oxygen masks on yourself first. There is no way to serve those around you when you are suffering. You can't give to others what you are lacking.

Hence the expression "hurt people hurt people." Pain is a vicious cycle that affects everyone. When you are broken, your sharp edges will most likely end up cutting someone. This can lead to more anguish, especially when you've hurt those you love.

The good news is that God heals you in ways you aren't even aware of. When you are sincere about your struggles—not only with God but with others—God's truth is able to restore you. When you are whole, you can then encounter the joy that comes from showing others that God revived you. Hurt people do, in fact, hurt people, but healed people can also heal people.

Which will you choose today?

• •

Lord, thank You for the complete and total healing that You paid for on the cross. Help me share the ways You've reconciled me so that others can see Your glory.

Thrill

And the God of all grace, who called you to his eternal glory
in Christ, after you have suffered a little while, will himself
restore you and make you strong, firm and steadfast.

1 PETER 5:10 NIV

Roller coaster enthusiasts will seek out the excitement of a theme park's newest ride. They spend hours in line in order to be one of the first to experience the hair-raising twists and turns. The crazier the ride, the more they savor it. Meanwhile, the average person stares at them, bewildered.

The ups and downs of life can be scarier than any roller coaster. Not knowing what to expect is frustrating and alarming. The speed of change can leave your stomach reeling. You sit there holding on, knuckles white, just hoping the horrible situation ends soon.

The suffering of this world is unavoidable, but the grace of God is sufficient for you. Whatever you might be faced with, He will use it to make you strong. When you can't find solid ground, you can stand firm in Him and rejoice that He will personally restore you. Life might be an unwanted thrill ride, but when God is next to you, the joy He brings is a thrill.

Lord, the circumstance I am going through is taking
me for a ride. Thank You for not only staying with
me but giving me joy in the midst of trials.

Wake Up

For anything that becomes visible is light.
Therefore it says, "Awake, O sleeper, and arise
from the dead, and Christ will shine on you."
EPHESIANS 5:14 ESV

• •

Bears do multiple things to stay safe while hibernating. They start by creating their den at the perfect elevation. They also make it small enough for their body heat to keep them warm. And finally, they make sure they've stored enough fat to sustain them through the winter. They protect themselves because sleep puts the body in a vulnerable state.

It can be tempting to snooze your way through life. Try as you might, you don't see any reason to get up. You have your own problems, and seeing the pain that others are in makes you feel listless. Shutting off your alarm and staying in bed seems the only feasible solution.

When you answer God's call, however, you instantly wake up. The pain of others doesn't cause you to shy away but compels you to show His love to them. The need to ignore the reality of a situation becomes less important than helping someone endure it. If you hear the Holy Spirit and choose not to ignore, indescribable joy is yours. All you have to do is wake up.

• •

Father God, I don't want to ignore the hostile
environment around me—I want to answer Your call
to soothe it. Help me dispense Your mercy and love.

Adrenaline

For we do not have a high priest who is unable to empathize with our weaknesses, but we have one who has been tempted in every way, just as we are—yet he did not sin.
HEBREWS 4:15 NIV

. . . .

Many adrenaline junkies love skydiving. The rush of feel-good chemicals that get released as they plummet toward the earth is addicting. If you were forced to skydive, however, you'd probably be less excited. At the very least, you'd want to talk to some experts first.

Life can be even more frightening and anxiety inducing than skydiving. Unexpected tragedies, difficult situations, unlovable people—you never know what terrors lie around each corner. You've heard of circumstances similar to yours, but if anyone really understood, your response wouldn't surprise them.

Hearing someone say, "Oh, I went through the same thing," can be painful, but when God says that, you can have joy that He actually means it. Jesus came to earth and went through a gamut of emotions, so you can know God empathizes with you. The adrenaline that comes from being understood by the Creator of the universe is better than any free fall.

. . . .

Father God, there might not be anything new under the sun, but this trouble is new to me. I give it to You and trust that Your wisdom will lead me to joy.

Where Did You Get That?

*Let love and faithfulness never leave you; bind
them around your neck, write them on the tablet
of your heart. Then you will win favor and a
good name in the sight of God and man.*

PROVERBS 3:3–4 NIV

. . . .

When you see a woman with a beautiful necklace on, one of the first
things you ask her is where she got it. You automatically think of all the
outfits you own that would be even cuter if you had that same necklace.
As soon as you get the chance, you are definitely going to go get one.

As many compliments as jewelry might attract, however, wearing
love and faithfulness will ensure you receive even more. Maintaining
these virtues can be hard, though. With all the pressures you are faced
with, consistently showing love and faithfulness is demanding.

When you are short on love and faithfulness, you can have joy that
Jesus is your perfect source and example. While it might be challenging
to hold yourself to these standards, God will enable you because He
expects it of you. When you love the Lord and are faithful to Him,
others can't help but notice.

And it won't be a problem telling them where you got it.

. . . .

*God, I want to be a good example of Your love and
faithfulness. In each interaction I have with others,
please help me remember I am Your child.*

Reservations

See how very much our Father loves us, for he calls us
his children, and that is what we are! But the people
who belong to this world don't recognize that we
are God's children because they don't know him.

1 JOHN 3:1 NLT

If you were to make reservations at a five-star restaurant, you would expect a wonderful evening. As you walked into the dining room, you would say your name and expect to be seated. But imagine how flabbergasted you'd feel if they couldn't find your reservation!

When you make plans for your life and watch them fall through, it can feel like unkept reservations. The disappointment you have to deal with on a regular basis is disheartening. Why can't things just go smoothly whenever you've put forth so much effort?

When you make a commitment to God, His response is to call you His child. The love He has for you is so great that He calls you His own. You can rejoice that even if people can't recognize your worth, Jesus' sacrifice has made you worthy. It doesn't matter if your reservations are kept—your name is in the Lamb's book of life.

Lord, I am so grateful to be Your child. Help me minister to those
who don't know You, and may I not be hurt when I am rejected.

Everlasting

For this I toil, struggling with all his energy
that he powerfully works within me.

COLOSSIANS 1:29 ESV

• •

Seeing a child's unrestrained energy can make you acutely aware of how tired you are. If only you had a quarter of their passion, you'd be able to double your to-do list and finish it by sundown. Every day would seem full of possibilities and new opportunities because you would not feel so spent.

When you don't have energy, it's hard to brush your teeth, let alone accomplish what might be on the docket for the day. Trying to reach any goal takes about as much stamina as climbing Everest. It's not that you don't want to work for what you want—you just feel like your dreams have atrophied.

God placed desires in your heart for a reason. . .and it was not to wear you out. Whenever you are weary in trying to fulfill your vision, find where it has veered from God's desire for you. His Spirit can give you the enthusiasm you need to see your God-given aspirations come to pass. Once these dreams are accomplished and God has received the glory, your joy will be full. The spark He creates in you is everlasting.

• •

Lord, help me return to the purpose and desire You have
for me. My version leaves me feeling burnt out. I ask for
Your energy to fulfill the plans You have for me.

Surprise!

Since, then, you have been raised with Christ, set your hearts on things above, where Christ is, seated at the right hand of God. Set your minds on things above, not on earthly things.

COLOSSIANS 3:1–2 NIV

If you were given a gift, wrapped nicely with a pretty bow, you would want to know what is inside. It wouldn't make sense to set it in a corner somewhere and forget about it. If you did have to wait, though, you'd be thinking the whole time about the surprise inside.

Humans are gifted with the ability to not only self-reflect but change what they happen to be reflecting on. Whatever you set your mind on decides what type of experience you will have. While venting has its place, you don't want to adopt a passive mindset concerning your struggles.

Your anger and frustration are real, but God is always good. Speaking about what God has done for you—and what He will continue to do—is not disregarding reality. Rather, changing your attention to Him will make way for joy. Use your gift and shift your focus today. What you find will be a pleasant surprise!

Father God, it can be hard to control my thoughts, especially when I am struggling. Help me have gratitude as I concentrate on Your Word.

Women Included

Accept one another, then, just as Christ accepted
you, in order to bring praise to God.
ROMANS 15:7 NIV

. . . .

What is clear to God isn't always clear to everyone else. The Bible explains that God's thoughts and ways are far above anyone else's (Isaiah 55:8–9). It is imperative that we keep from misinterpreting His words through our personal or cultural bias.

Priscilla (a woman) and her husband, Aquila, worked together to help Paul and further the cause of the kingdom. In his letters, Paul also mentioned Junia (a woman who was imprisoned alongside him for preaching the gospel), so that she would be noted among the apostles. Euodia (a woman) and Syntyche (a woman) also worked with him to spread the gospel. The list could go on.

There is a thought that women don't have a place in church leadership, but that contradicts the hundreds of verses about women who excelled in leadership for God's kingdom. Men and women can partner together and bring glory to God. You can rejoice—all women, including you, have a place!

When the Holy Spirit is at work in someone, that person mustn't remain silent. Women included.

. . . .

Lord, I ask for revival in the hearts of the leaders
of the church. Thank You for giving everyone
opportunity to share the truth of who You are.

Pick Him

Better is one day in your courts than a thousand elsewhere; I would rather be a doorkeeper in the house of my God than dwell in the tents of the wicked.

PSALM 84:10 NIV

When you are presented with opposing views, you feel pressured to choose one. Many of these choices are trivial, such as whether you drink coffee or tea. Other topics, however, can be a bit more divisive. These hot-button issues can be a burden on you and your relationships, splitting everyone into different camps.

It doesn't matter which side you select—your decision will lead to several other issues. Arguments may start replacing pleasant conversation. Negative emotions can well up as you compare your righteousness to others' obvious ignorance. Being "right" can be a hard burden to bear.

Fortunately, you don't have to stay in the camps of bitterness and resentment. There's a third option, which is the house of the Lord. Where He dwells, there is unity, love, and peace. When you serve God, you can have joy knowing you are outside of the strife. When Jesus is your choice, no other options are worth considering.

Lord, there will always be subjects that will alienate me from others. I thank You that Your presence brings unity, and I ask You to help me function in the friction.

Great Things

You thrill me, LORD, with all you have done for me!
I sing for joy because of what you have done.
PSALM 92:4 NLT

. . . .

Sarah had wanted a baby, but she was old, and she and Abraham weren't getting any younger. She had come to terms with the fact that her dream had passed her by. But then the Lord visited her, promising she would have a child! Sarah and Abraham would end up naming their son Isaac, which means laughter—a perfect response to such an unexpected surprise.

The Bible clearly tells all God has done for you. He sent His Son to die as a payment for sin on the cross. He rose again, conquering hell, death, and the grave. There is a place being built just for you in heaven. And today, His Holy Spirit is here to surround you and give you comfort.

But God doesn't stop there. Just as God gave Sarah the joy of an unexpected surprise, He can bless you when you least expect it. You are not too old—or too young—to be blessed by God. And when it happens, you too will sing for joy because He has done great things.

. . . .

Father God, I will not put a limit on Your use for me.
Help me listen to Your Spirit and trust in Your perfect timing.

Revel

*But Joseph said to them, "Don't be afraid. Am I
in the place of God? You intended to harm me,
but God intended it for good to accomplish what
is now being done, the saving of many lives."*
GENESIS 50:19–20 NIV

. . . .

Joseph's brothers were so angry with him that they sold him to the
Midianite merchants. Joseph would go on to be the head of a pharaoh
official's household, spend roughly ten years in prison, and finally
become vice-regent to the pharaoh himself. In this position, he would
save countless lives from famine.

When his brothers found out that the man who had saved them
from starvation was the brother they'd tried to get rid of, they were
terrified. Joseph responded by telling them not to be afraid, because
God had intended it all for good. Joseph understood that he was not
God. . .and that what God wants gets priority.

Vitriol from others is hard to deal with; however, God can use it
to benefit you, just like He did with Joseph. It might be tempting to
lash out and wreak vengeance, but you don't have to. You can rejoice
knowing that God will handle them and work everything for your good.

A reckoning isn't as fun as reveling in the power of God in your life.

. . . .

*Lord, even when I feel like I'm an outcast, I will continue
to seek You. I trust that no matter how irreparable the
situation might seem, You will use it for good.*

Shine Bright

"In the same way, let your light shine before others, that they may see your good deeds and glorify your Father in heaven."
MATTHEW 5:16 NIV

Not everyone was born in the same time period as you; therefore, it is special to you—and about seven billion other people. Regardless of whether you were born in this age or not, there will always be some darkness to battle. As you grow up and learn more about the world, you become aware of exactly how murky it can get.

There is no shortage of bad news. Calamity and death are available at every turn. People are marginalized, overlooked, or completely forgotten about. Loss runs rampant. Things are constantly breaking, and nothing seems to last. True commitment is hard to come by. All of these things can leave you feeling depressed and powerless.

God saved you so that you can be a light unto a dark world. A light does not complain about the dark—it drives it out. You can decide to let God shine through you so that others can start to see. Others will rejoice that they can see what was hidden from them, and you can share in their joy.

The times that you're living in are dark, but that's all the more reason to shine bright.

Lord, the darkness of human nature is not new.
Thank You for shining Your light through me so
that others may see You more clearly.

Overcome

But this I call to mind, and therefore I have
hope: The steadfast love of the LORD never
ceases; his mercies never come to an end.
LAMENTATIONS 3:21–22 ESV

Have you ever had trouble remembering something important? Perhaps while reminiscing about a past event with friends, you learned that it didn't quite happen like you thought. Or maybe you forgot where you put your car keys, purse, files, or baby's pacifier, thus causing your day to be ruined.

It is interesting how you can forget something you need but remember things you truly don't want to. It'd be amazing if you could sort out all the unwanted images and interactions stored in your memory bank, but it appears they aren't going anywhere. Those recollections pop up at the most inconvenient times, bringing a lot of pain with them.

In these situations, the Holy Spirit is there to remind you of the all-consuming love of the Lord. Still, you have to actively call to mind what God has said not only about you but about Himself. Write down all that the Lord has done for you. When you look back at His mercy, you will be overcome with joy.

Lord, I will hide Your Word in my heart so that I can combat
my thoughts. I will recall all that You've done for me and praise
You for it so that I can overcome the battles in my mind.

Give It Away

One gives freely, yet grows all the richer; another
withholds what he should give, and only suffers
want. Whoever brings blessing will be enriched,
and one who waters will himself be watered.

PROVERBS 11:24–25 ESV

Whenever the possibility of a natural disaster (such as a hurricane) starts looming—or when an item becomes scarce—people tend to buy more than they need. It can be extremely uncomfortable to find yourself without the things you need. People naturally try to prepare themselves for uncertainty.

It's possible to withhold and store nonmaterial items as well. If you've been hurt before, you may not give out love as freely. People have to meet a checklist before you open up. Others have abused your time so much that you hold precious each moment you have to yourself. The idea of volunteering for anything is ludicrous.

Giving items to others in need is a great place to begin. . .but that's not where a follower of Jesus should stop. When you give freely of your time and show God's love toward others, the blessings are immense. The joy you crave comes when you give freely.

Love isn't just a thought or feeling—it's a treasure to be given.

Father God, help me try my best to meet the needs of others.
What grace has given me, help me let it flow to others.

Come Forth

Instead, be very glad—for these trials make you
partners with Christ in his suffering, so that
you will have the wonderful joy of seeing his
glory when it is revealed to all the world.

1 PETER 4:13 NLT

When Jesus told Lazarus to come forth from his grave, not everyone was happy. His sisters, Mary and Martha, were ecstatic, of course, but the Pharisees were not. They not only wanted Jesus gone; they sought to destroy Lazarus as well. He was walking around sharing his testimony of what the Lord had done, causing other people to follow Christ.

It can be tempting not to share your testimony of how you came to follow the Lord, especially when you don't know how it will be received. Going to church on Sunday and worshipping alongside other Christians seems enough. You've heard some amazing accounts of redemption, and you don't want to be mocked by others for your story.

People need to know how Jesus turned your life around, and it is okay if you get ridiculed for it. That never stopped Jesus, and it doesn't have to stop you. As you share your story, His glory will be revealed and your joy will be complete.

There is no need to hesitate—go ahead and come forth!

Lord, help me shout out all that You've rescued me
from. I don't want to keep quiet—there are too
many who need to hear about Your greatness.

Forever

We do not look at the things that can be seen.
We look at the things that cannot be seen.
The things that can be seen will come to an end.
But the things that cannot be seen will last forever.

2 CORINTHIANS 4:18 NLV

. . . .

Regardless of how well something is preserved, it will eventually crumble and fade. As protected and maintained as the *Mona Lisa* is, nothing will be able to save it from the slow march of time. This is true for anything that can be seen or touched.

It's not wise to let visible, temporary, changeable things control your life. The reflection you see in the mirror will change. Something you love and use every day will eventually wear out. Whatever it might be, if you can see and touch it, time will alter it.

God is not bound by time, so He remains unchanged. When you look at Him, you are beholding that which has no end. You can rejoice that though everything around you may waste away, the God you worship remains steadfast. Don't concern yourself with what is finite. Artworks and buildings might be lost to history, but the redemption of the Lord lasts forever.

. . . .

God, forever is an awfully long time. . .so I want to spend
it with You. Help me be mindful of what will further
Your kingdom because the joy in that is endless.

Soul

"And what do you benefit if you gain the whole world but lose your own soul? Is anything worth more than your soul?"
MATTHEW 16:26 NLT

. . . .

The only word that describes what you feel is *uncomfortable*. Feeling confined can lead to a plethora of problems. Life loses its luster. Anxiety and depression envelop all other emotions. Worst of all, you feel completely dissatisfied when you look in the mirror.

Knowing that no one will understand, you feel alone. Your family and friends go merrily about their life, leaving you feeling like a mistake. If God didn't get it wrong, then in your opinion, He has an awful sense of humor.

The reason you feel the way you do is because who you are is a lot more than what you see in a reflection. Your appearance is less important than your soul. The joy you experience when you give yourself to God far outweighs the limits of your body. If something plagues your thoughts—like a hangnail in your heart—lay it at the feet of Jesus. Nothing should grip your soul's attention like Jesus' love. Your body won't last forever but your soul will.

. . . .

*Father God, I know this body is temporary. Help me
have a deeper understanding of Your love for me so
that I can accept myself and focus on eternity.*

Whistle While You Work

"And I will make an everlasting covenant with them: I will never stop doing good for them. . . . I will find joy doing good for them and will faithfully and wholeheartedly replant them in this land."

<small>JEREMIAH 32:40–41 NLT</small>

. . . .

If only you could do the things you have to do with a good attitude, your whole life would go much more smoothly. There would be no dread when the alarm clock sounded for you to get up and go to work—you would be pleased to do so. It wouldn't stress you out to have your family ask you what dinner will be—you would be honored to make it.

Obligations can be a burden. The exhaustion that comes from daily commitments borders on clinical fatigue. Some days, you can do it with a smile on your face; other days, the weight of it leaves you in tears.

Unlike you and everyone else, God has no problem keeping His word. . .and He is happy to do so. Not only is God good and dedicated to doing good, He actually rejoices in doing good for you. God enjoys working in your best interest, and that means helping you accomplish hard things.

Rejoice in Him, and you'll find yourself whistling while you work.

. . . .

Father God, when I am feeling overwhelmed by my responsibilities, remind me to rejoice in You. You are the author of life, and all that You establish is good.

Inheritance

*"And now I entrust you to God and the message of
his grace that is able to build you up and give you an
inheritance with all those he has set apart for himself."*

ACTS 20:32 NLT

A last will and testament is extremely important in carrying out the wishes of the testator, who is the person making the will. The testator has thought extensively about who will receive the benefits of that person's life's work—so much so that the testator has the proper documents drawn up so that no one can dispute them.

The Bible is a testament, and it shows the will of God for all of His children. When Jesus died, it released the promises of the kingdom to you. Because you are a child of God, you have the ability to partake in all that He has offered you. All that He has is yours because of Jesus.

The best part is that your benefactor, God, is still very much alive. Both you and God can have joy when you take part in the legacy He wants you to continue. The fruits of the Spirit—and so much more— are yours.

Since Jesus is alive, you don't have to wait—you can use your inheritance now.

*Father God, I am so grateful I am Your child. Help
me use my inheritance to show Your love to others and
let them know what a good Father You are.*

Scripture Index

More Inspiration for Your Lovely Heart

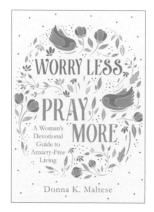

This purposeful devotional guide features 180 readings and prayers designed to help alleviate your worries as you learn to live in the peace of the Almighty God, who offers calm for your anxiety-filled soul. Worry Less, Pray More reinforces the truth that, with God, you can live anxiety-free every single day—whether you worry about your work, relationships, bills, the turmoil of the world, or something more.

Paperback/978-1-68322-861-5